MW00489754

SPECIAL APPLICATIONS
OF REBT

Joseph Yankura, Ph.D., is a psychologist in private practice in Merrick, New York. He is also a school psychologist in Long Beach, New York, and an adjunct clinical supervisor for the doctoral program in clinical psychology at the C. W. Post campus of Long Island University. He has co-authored five books with Windy Dryden, including *Daring to Be Myself: A Case Study in Rational-Emotive Therapy, Counselling Individuals: A Rational-Emotive Handbook* (2nd ed.), and *Developing Rational-Emotive Behavioral Counselling.* His current interests lie in developing disorder-specific REBT treatment manuals, and in refining cognitive-behavioral treatments for anxiety disorders.

Windy Dryden, Ph.D., is Professor of Counseling at Goldsmiths College, University of London. He edits twelve book series in the areas of counseling and psychotherapy, and has published over one-hundred books (including *The Practice of REBT,* co-authored with Albert Ellis). His major interests are in developing the theory and practice of REBT, and in eclecticism and integration in psychotherapy.

SPECIAL APPLICATIONS OF REBT

A Therapist's Casebook

Joseph Yankura, PhD
Windy Dryden, PhD
Editors

 Springer Publishing Company

Copyright © 1997 by Springer Publishing Company, Inc.

All rights reserved

No part of this publication may be reproduced, stored in a retrieval
system, or transmitted in any form or by any means, electronic, mechanical,
photocopying, recording, or otherwise, without the prior permission of
Springer Publishing Company, Inc.

Springer Publishing Company, Inc.
536 Broadway
New York, NY 10012-3955

Cover design by Margaret Dunin
Acquisitions Editor: Bill Tucker
Production Editor: Jeanne Libby

97 98 99 00 01 / 5 4 3 2 1

Library of Congress Cataloging-in-Publication-Data

Special applications of REBT: a therapist's casebook / Joseph
  Yankura, Windy Dryden, editors.
        p.   cm.
    Includes bibliographical references and index.
    ISBN 0-8261-9801-5
    1. Rational-emotive psychotherapy.   I. Yankura, Joseph.
  II. Dryden, Windy.
    [DNLM: 1. Psychotherapy, Rational-Emotive.   2. Psychotherapy,
  Group.   WM 420.5.P8 S741   1997]
  RC489.R3S64   1997
  616.89'14—dc21
  DNLM/DLC
  for Library of Congress   97-23193
                                                                  CIP

Printed in the United States of America

Contents

Contributors   *vii*

1 Introduction   1
        Joseph Yankura and Windy Dryden

2 Applications of REBT with Children and Adolescents   11
        Ann Vernon

3 *"Shoya Moya Ik Baraba":* Using REBT with Culturally
        Diverse Clients   39
        Mitchell W. Robin and Raymond DiGiuseppe

4 Using REBT with Clients with Disabilities   69
        Rochelle Balter

5 Rational-Emotive Family Therapy   101
        Charles H. Huber

6 REBT and Its Application to Group Therapy   131
        Albert Ellis

7 Conclusion   163
        Joseph Yankura and Windy Dryden

Index   *173*

Contributors

Rochelle Balter, Ph.D., is a psychologist in private practice in New York City, and also serves on the consulting staff of the Chronic Fatigue Crisis Center. She was the 1996 Chair of the APA Committee on Disability Issues in Psychology, and is one of the coordinators of Psychologists with Disabilities. She is co-author (with Mitchell W. Robin, Ph.D.) of the self-help book, *Performance Anxiety.*

Raymond DiGiuseppe, PhD, is Professor of Psychology at St. John's University in New York City, and Director of Professional Education at the Institute for Rational-Emotive Therapy. He has published over 60 journal articles and book chapters, and has coauthored 5 books (including *A Practitioner's Guide to Rational-Emotive Therapy*). His present work is focused on the assessment and treatment of anger problems and the treatment of externalizing disorders in children and adolescents.

Albert Ellis, Ph.D., is the creator and primary exponent of REBT. He is President of the Institute for Rational-Emotive Therapy in New York City, and has authored more than seven-hundred articles and over fifty books. His recent books include *Reason and Emotion in Psychotherapy, Revised and Updated* and *Better, Deeper, and More Enduring Brief Therapy.*

Charles H. Huber, Ph.D., is a Professor in the Department of Counseling and Educational Psychology at New Mexico State University, Las Cruces. He has published numerous articles in professional journals, and has co-authored (with Leroy Baruth, Ed.D.) several books on marital and family therapy. These titles include *Rational-Emotive Family Therapy: A Systems Perspective.*

Mitchell W. Robin, Ph.D., is Professor of Psychology at New York City Technical College of the City University of New York. He has been actively involved in research on the impact of culture on the endorsement of irrational beliefs, the mental health of the client, and the client's response to psychotherapy. He is co-author (with Rochelle Balter, Ph.D.) of the self-help book, *Performance Anxiety.*

Ann Vernon, Ph.D., is Professor and Coordinator of Counseling in the Department of Educational Administration and Counseling at the University of Northern Iowa, Cedar Falls. She is Director of the Midwest Center for Rational-Emotive Therapy, and the author of numerous journal articles and books. Her books include *Thinking, Feeling, Behaving: Emotional Education Curriculums for Children and Adolescents* and *Counseling Children and Adolescents.*

CHAPTER 1

Introduction

Joseph Yankura and Windy Dryden

The chapters comprising the present volume are intended to describe and illustrate (through provision of actual case material) special applications of rational emotive behavior therapy (REBT). Specifically, the reader will see how REBT can be used with (1) children and adolescents, (2) culturally diverse clients, (3) clients with disabilities, (4) families, and (5) ongoing therapy groups.

REBT possesses a number of features that allow it to be effectively applied to a wide range of special populations and therapeutic modalities. In particular, we would note that REBT:

Offers a model for conceptualizing and addressing emotional and behavioral problems that can be readily learned by many clients. REBT practitioners function, in part, as "psychological educators," and they typically teach their clients a number of concepts and skills that can enable them to ultimately act as their own therapists. In particular, clients are taught how to (a) analyze episodes of emotional and behavioral disturbance with REBT's ABC model; (b) discriminate between irrational and rational beliefs; (c) distinguish healthy (or appropriate) negative emotions from unhealthy (or inappropriate) negative emotions; and (d) utilize a variety of means for modifying the irrational beliefs that underpin their emotional and behavioral problems. The manner in which these concepts and skills are presented to clients can be creatively modified in a number of different ways,

1

such that even relatively psychologically unsophisticated or cognitively limited individuals can apply and benefit from them. Unlike some alternative approaches to therapy (such as classical psychoanalysis), REBT shows clients that the roots of their disturbance can be readily accessed and (with consistent effort) remediated.

Because its essentials can be learned fairly easily by many clients, REBT lends itself quite well to applications within self-help and conventional therapy groups wherein the participants actively attempt to render meaningful assistance to one another. Group participants are, in effect, able to act in the role of therapist for each other.

Is flexible with respect to choice of intervention strategies and techniques. REBT especially focuses on helping clients to replace their dysfunctional cognitions with more helpful ones, and offers them a variety of techniques for accomplishing this task. Chief among these techniques is philosophical disputing. However, this particular cognitive method requires that the client be able to self-monitor for irrational beliefs and engage in a fair amount of abstract thinking. As such, it is often not appropriate for intellectually limited individuals or younger children. When REBT therapists work with such clients they try to provide more appropriate, alternative techniques for promoting cognitive change, such as regular (and vigorous!) practice of rational self-statements (Dryden & Yankura, 1993; Ellis, 1979). These self-statements are often developed collaboratively by client and therapist, and furnish the client with rational messages intended to counter specific irrational beliefs to which he or she subscribes.

In addition to being flexible with respect to techniques for effecting cognitive change, REBT is also *generally* flexible with respect to intervention strategies. Thus, if a given client fails to benefit from methods aimed at effecting profound philosophical change, the REBT therapist will explore other strategies for helping the individual to make progress with presenting problems. Such strategies may include attempts to facilitate inferentially based change, behaviorally based change, or modifications to the client's negative Activating Events. REBT espouses a strong *preference* for techniques that will help clients to effect change at the philosophical level, but REBT therapists refrain from making this preference into a *must* and will strike therapeutic compromises when these are called for (see Dryden, 1991a; for further discussion on the issue of compromises in REBT).

Since REBT is flexible with respect to choice of change strategies and techniques, it is able to provide meaningful therapeutic assistance to a broad array of client types. We would note, however, that REBT therapists work from a consistent theoretical base that guides their selection of intervention strategies, and will eschew methods and techniques that have the potential to inadvertently reinforce clients' irrational philosophies (Dryden, 1991b; Ellis, 1982, 1983).

Clearly elucidates the therapeutic vehicles which potentially can lead to improved psychological functioning for clients. One of the first things that REBT therapists will teach to their clients is the important link between Beliefs (Bs) and emotional and behavioral Consequences (Cs). In fact, REBT therapists will generally refrain from proceeding with actual intervention strategies (such as philosophical disputing) until clients see and understand the B→C relationship (Dryden & Yankura, 1995). Once this relationship is understood, they are explicitly taught that challenging and replacing their irrational beliefs represents a most important means for minimizing disturbance and facilitating improved psychological functioning. As such, the route to therapeutic progress is openly revealed to clients, and they are not left wondering just how therapy is supposed to help them. This explicit approach to teaching about change strategies may make REBT appealing to individuals who would avoid entering or persisting with other sorts of therapies because they have difficulty comprehending the manner in which they are intended to be helpful. Since REBT is quite clear about the mechanisms by which change is to be implemented, it mitigates against clients becoming disillusioned and dropping out of treatment due to confusion as to how they are to improve and what they are to do in order to bring about this improvement.

Can help clients to begin experiencing meaningful improvements in a relatively brief span of time. Since REBT is a problem-focused approach to treatment and REBT therapists tend to adopt an active-directive stance with most of their clients (Dryden & Yankura, 1993), the actual "work" of therapy quite often begins during the very first session. As a result, clients can frequently be helped to experience some relief from their upsets relatively soon after their treatment has started. To cite an example, a client suffering from guilt and depression can swiftly be shown that the negative self-rating she is engaging in is unnecessary and unwarranted insofar as it is both illogical and empirically unsound. Once able to see this, she may be able to experience some positive changes in her affect. Granted, such swift change will likely be transient, as it usually takes time and effort for clients to accomplish meaningful philosophic change. Nevertheless, it can serve to bolster hope, strengthen client confidence in the treatment being offered, and facilitate motivation to become fully engaged in therapy. Once again, clients may be more likely to become discouraged and disillusioned with therapeutic approaches that delay the actual "start" of therapy with extensive psychological testing and history-taking, or that purport to promote change through a very gradual accretion of presumably helpful "insights."

Refrains from challenging the client's perceptions of "reality." When clients first arrive for therapy, they will quite often provide their therapist with a description of negative circumstances that they see as implicated in their emotional and behavioral problems. From the REBT perspective, they are, in effect, describing their negative Activating Events (As). These descriptions are typically not pure, objective portrayals of events and circumstances confronting the client; rather, they usually include the clients' inferences about these events and circumstances. Here, the term "inferences" is used to encompass the interpretations, attributions, and predictions that an individual makes about personally meaningful events and circumstances.

While many alternative approaches to cognitive-behavior therapy would begin actual treatment by examining and challenging any faulty negative inferences that the client may appear to have, REBT therapists will accept (at least initially) the client's description of A as if it were true, and will instead focus their efforts at uncovering (and ultimately disputing) the client's irrational demands and evaluative cognitions *about* that particular A (Dryden & DiGiuseppe, 1990). To cite an example, a given client might arrive for therapy complaining of anxiety related to her view that her boss doesn't like her and wants to fire her. A good number of cognitive-behavior therapists would respond to such a complaint with a line of questioning intended to help the client consider alternative (and presumably more accurate and less upset-provoking) interpretations of the way her boss seems to act toward her. The REBT therapist, on the other hand, would tend to make the following sort of statement to the client: "Let's suppose it's true that your boss dislikes you and would like to fire you. Now, let's examine what you're telling yourself *about* this situation to bring on your anxiety!"

This stance toward dealing with client descriptions of A stems directly from REBT's view of the types of cognitions centrally implicated in bringing on emotional disturbance. Irrational beliefs—generally viewed as consisting of an absolutistic demand and an absolutistic evaluative conclusion—are accorded primacy in the genesis of disturbance (Dryden & DiGiuseppe, 1990). As such, identifying and modifying these beliefs is a major focus of rational emotive behavioral treatment. Negatively distorted inferences are not accorded a central role; instead, they are viewed as actually stemming from the irrational beliefs to which an individual subscribes (Ellis, 1995).

While research suggests that cognitive-behavioral interventions which focus on challenging faulty inferences have considerable clinical utility, it must be noted that these interventions have typically been tested with the "traditional" client pools tapped for treatment outcome research (e.g., college students; mental health center clients). They have not, however, been put to the test with nontraditional samples, such as culturally diverse clients. Conceivably, it is possible that some individuals will see attempts to dispute their inferences as challenges to their view of reality, and they may have a negative response to this. This issue may have particular relevance when the client comes from a cultural background dissimilar to that of the therapist, and is sensitive to any signs that the therapist "just doesn't understand her." In scenarios like this, it may be the case that REBT offers a particular advantage, as it doesn't hasten to challenge the client's view of reality. Instead, it conveys to the client that his or her view is accepted, and offers to help the client to become less vulnerable to upsets about the reality with which he or she has to deal.

These are some of the main aspects of REBT which, in our view, endow it with such broad applicability. We trust that other aspects will become evident as you proceed through the chapters comprising this book. Therefore, without further ado, let us provide you with an overview of the present volume's contents.

Chapter 2, by Ann Vernon, provides a comprehensive overview of REBT's application with children and adolescents. She provides a rationale for using REBT with young clients, and then proceeds to discuss issues pertaining to problem conceptualization and assessment, establishing the therapeutic relationship, assessment of irrational beliefs (including issues pertaining to the developmental level of the child client), and the REBT intervention process. Throughout these sections, she illustrates important concepts and techniques by describing the case of Nathan, a 16-year-old boy who was referred for counseling by his parents because of anxiety and depressed moods. She then proceeds to highlight how REBT can be effectively used for two particular emotional problems experienced by young clients: anger and anxiety. Overall, Vernon's chapter provides much useful information for practitioners wishing to refine the therapeutic work they do with children and youth.

In Chapter 3, Mitchell Robin and Raymond DiGiuseppe discuss utilization of REBT with culturally diverse clients. Their contribution can be considered particularly important and timely because, as they note, "In an ever widening multicultural environment it is a rare practitioner who is not confronted, at least occasionally, with a client who comes from a different background than herself." Robin and DiGiuseppe underscore the challenges of doing cross-cultural therapy, and present arguments in support of their view that REBT and other cognitive-behavioral therapies represent the most appropriate forms of treatment for culturally diverse clients. They then provide salient recommendations for deploying REBT with individuals whose cultural background differs from that of the therapist, and finally present the illustrative case of A.Z., a 32-year-old man from the Indian subcontinent who was seen in therapy by the first author. They conclude their chapter by reminding the reader that developing sensitivity to culturally diverse clients is best viewed as an ongoing process. By way of facilitating this process, they include a list of useful articles and books for therapists interested in pursuing further relevant reading.

Rochelle Balter details REBT's application with clients with disabilities in Chapter 4. She first provides a general introduction concerning important factors for therapists to be mindful of when working with clients with disabilities, and then underscores a number of issues of particular relevance to the REBT practitioner. She especially emphasizes the desirability of the therapist taking steps to deal with her own personal preconceptions and stereotypes, in order to ensure that the client with a disability is an active collaborator in the REBT treatment process. She highlights the fact that it can be relatively easy for therapists to bring negative biases about persons with disabilities to the treatment setting, with the result that problems are misidentified and the client is viewed as being unable to meaningfully participate in her own treatment. Balter then describes her therapeutic work with Helga, a 40-year-old woman whom she helped come to terms with the reality of having a physical disability. While the therapy was complex insofar as it addressed quite a number of issues, Helga made significant progress and was able to begin expanding areas of her life that had previously been rather constricted.

In Chapter 5, Charles Huber presents his unique conceptualization of rational-emotive family therapy (REFT). His approach to family treatment incorporates the family systems perspective, and thus diverges from "traditional" REBT in a number of important respects. In particular, Huber's version of REFT includes emphases on circular causality, the simultaneity of the elements of interactions between family members, and the identification of family beliefs. Huber notes that families are belief-governed systems, and that the "governing principles of family life" can be discerned through the repetitive patterns of behavior that exist among and between family members. He discusses differences between rational and irrational family beliefs, and provides details on problem conceptualization, assessment, and treatment according to his REFT model. Then, he illustrates enactment of REFT by describing the treatment of a family consisting of a husband and wife and their 14-year-old daughter. In the concluding discussion of his chapter, Huber points out how identification and modification of an irrational belief commonly held by all family members—as opposed to separately identifying and addressing the irrational beliefs held by individual family members—has the potential for greatly simplifying the treatment process by reducing the number of problem-relevant variables that have to be considered.

Albert Ellis describes the application of REBT to group therapy in Chapter 6. He begins his chapter by noting a number of the advantages of rational-emotive group therapy relative to rational-emotive individual therapy, and then continues on to detail the particulars of REBT groups. The different types of groups run at the Institute for Rational-Emotive Therapy in New York City are described, as well as the screening process for group members and the general procedures used for structuring regular group sessions. A comprehensive catalog of REBT group techniques is then provided, followed by the REBT approach to group processes. Ellis then presents the case of Barbara, a 36-year-old woman who entered one of the Institute's groups because of problems with social anxiety, nonassertiveness, and depression. After participating in the group for somewhat over a year, she had made significant progress with respect to her presenting problems.

The present volume concludes with an annotated bibliography containing sources which further illustrate REBT's applicability to various sorts of problems and types of clients. We included this bibliography for readers who wish to extend their study of REBT's many applications. Such readers are also referred to our other co-edited volume, *Using REBT with Common Psychological Problems: A Therapist's Casebook* (New York: Springer Publishing, 1997). This book illustrates REBT's application to the following clinical problems: (1) generalized anxiety disorder, (2) depression, (3) attention deficit/hyperactivity disorder, (4) panic disorder with agoraphobia, (5) anger and hostility, and (6) obsessive-compulsive disorder.

We would like to emphasize that this casebook is not intended to provide the reader with a basic foundation in the theory and practice of REBT. Readers wishing for this sort of material will find it helpful to consult *The Clinical Practice of Rational Emotive Behavior Therapy*, by Albert Ellis and Windy Dryden (New York: Springer Publishing, 1997). This book reviews fundamental REBT concepts and techniques, and describes steps for applying REBT to individuals, groups, and couples.

And now, on to the casebook chapters!

REFERENCES

Dryden, W. (1991a). Compromises in rational-emotive therapy. In W. Dryden (Ed.), *Reason and therapeutic change* (pp. 260–271). London: Whurr.

Dryden, W. (1991b). Rational-emotive therapy and eclecticism. In W. Dryden (Ed.), *Reason and therapeutic change* (pp. 272–279). London: Whurr.

Dryden, W., & DiGiuseppe, R. (1990). *A primer on rational-emotive therapy.* Champaign, IL: Research Press.

Dryden, W., & Yankura, J. (1993). *Counselling individuals: A rational-emotive handbook* (2nd ed.). London: Whurr.

Dryden, W., & Yankura, J. (1995). *Developing rational emotive behavioral counselling.* London: Sage.

Ellis, A. (1979). The practice of rational-emotive therapy. In A. Ellis & J. M. Whiteley (Eds.), *Theoretical and empirical foundations of rational-emotive therapy* (pp. 61–100). Monterey, CA: Brooks/Cole.

Ellis, A. (1982). Must most psychotherapists remain as incompetent as they now are? *Journal of Contemporary Psychotherapy, 13*(1), 17–28.

Ellis, A. (1983). The philosophic implications and dangers of some popular behavior therapy techniques. In M. Rosenbaum, C. M. Franks, & Y. Jaffe (Eds.), *Perspectives on behavior therapy in the eighties* (pp. 138–151). New York: Springer.

Ellis, A. (1995). Fundamentals of rational emotive behaviour therapy for the 1990s. In W. Dryden (Ed.), *Rational emotive behaviour therapy: A reader* (pp. 1–30). London: Sage.

Ellis, A., & Dryden, W. (1996). *The clinical practice of rational emotive behavior therapy.* New York: Springer.

Yankura, J., & Dryden, W. (Eds.). (1997). *Using REBT with common psychological problems: A therapist's casebook.* New York: Springer.

CHAPTER 2

Applications of REBT with Children and Adolescents

Ann Vernon

As an elementary school-aged child, I remember responding to classmates' teasing by taunting, "Sticks and stones can break my bones, but words will never hurt me." Despite having said this, I know that I didn't *believe* that words couldn't hurt me. Although the chanting of this phrase served as a type of defense against their insults, what I really needed was an *explanation* of why words didn't have to hurt, and how I could develop some "emotional muscle" to protect myself from these typical verbal slugs that characterize childhood and adolescence.

As professionals working with children and adolescents, we would like to believe that teasing and name-calling are among the worst problems young people experience. In reality, we know differently, as illustrated by the following statistics relative to what children in the United States experience (Wittmer, 1993, pp. 14–15):

- Every 47 seconds a child is abused or neglected.
- Every 7 minutes a child is killed or injured by guns.

- Every day 6 teenagers commit suicide.
- Every 14 hours a child younger than five is murdered.
- Every 5 hours a 15- to-19-year-old is murdered.
- Every 4 seconds of the school day a public school student is corporally punished.
- Every 26 seconds a child runs away from home.
- Every day 100,000 children are homeless.
- Every day 2,989 American children experience divorce in their families.
- Every 74 seconds a 15- to-19-year-old woman has an abortion.

In addition to these statistics, superimpose the normal problems which characterize middle childhood: Developing physical, emotional, and academic competence; establishing a place in a peer group; learning to deal with competition; and gaining self-confidence. In early adolescence, the challenge is greater as puberty kicks into gear and young adolescents find themselves riding on an emotional roller-coaster. Dealing with intense emotions, bodily changes, and peer group pressures are among the significant concerns. By midadolescence, teenagers are faced with another set of challenges: Confronting anxiety about post-high school plans; negotiating the intricacies of intimate relationship and sexuality issues; and wrestling with identity concerns.

Practitioners have become increasingly aware of the need for effective prevention and intervention strategies to help young clients cope with normal developmental stressors as well as with the infinite number of more serious familial or socioemotional problems which often result in self-defeating behaviors such as substance abuse, suicide, teen pregnancy, or violence (Vernon, 1993a; Wittmer, 1993). According to Bernard and Joyce (1984), this awareness began in the middle 1960s with the recognition that there were more factors which put children "at risk," and that the number of children demonstrating various forms of emotional and behavioral maladjustment was increasing. In addition, mental health professionals realized that simply extrapolating adult assessment and intervention strategies for use with children and adolescents was not effective practice (Vernon, 1993b). As a result, there has been a concerted effort in recent years to identify what constitutes effective prevention and intervention with young clients.

Professionals interested in the mental health of children are increasingly practicing rational emotive behavior therapy. As Bernard and Joyce (1984) noted after an extensive review of the literature, "There is now a sophisticated as well as a systematic procedure for employing RET with children and youth" (p. 26).

Rational emotive behavior therapy, formerly called rational-emotive therapy, was developed by Dr. Albert Ellis in 1955. Not long after he began using REBT with adults, Ellis realized that it could be effectively applied to children as well as to their parents. A number of important publications have described the use of REBT with children and adolescents (Barrish & Barrish, 1989; Bedford, 1974; Bernard & Joyce, 1984; DiGiuseppe, 1975, 1981; Ellis & Bernard, 1983; Ellis, Moseley & Wolfe, 1966; Hauck, 1967, 1983; Vernon, 1983; Waters, 1982; Wilde, 1992). In recent years, prevention programs based on rational-emotive principles have been developed (Knaus, 1974; Pincus, 1990; Vernon, 1989a, 1989b, 1989c; Waters, 1979, 1980). Rational emotive behavior therapy is currently being used with young clients in the United States and increasingly in Australia, England, Holland, and other Western European countries.

In this chapter, specific applications of rational emotive behavior therapy with children and adolescents will be described. Selected case studies will be used to illustrate concepts.

RATIONAL EMOTIVE BEHAVIOR THERAPY WITH CHILDREN: A RATIONALE

Unlike other forms of therapy, an integral part of REBT is its emphasis on teaching and prevention. Knaus (1974) described it as a therapeutic approach "by which children can be taught sane mental health concepts and the skills to use these concepts" (p. 1). Inherent in this definition is the notion that there are identifiable, concrete concepts which should be presented to children. While it may seem as if this is stating the obvious, most therapeutic approaches do not emphasize skill acquisition in a deliberate manner; thus, the concept of teaching mental health skills to children and adolescents is an important distinguishing feature of rational emotive behavior therapy.

What makes this therapeutic approach so practical with children and adolescents is the fact that a wide variety of cognitive, emotive, behavioral, kinesthetic, verbal, and oral assessment and intervention techniques can be employed. Given this latitude, the therapist is free to be very creative in adapting strategies to a younger population. Not only does this make the therapeutic process more interesting and engaging for both client and counselor, but it also allows the therapist to target the problem more specifically. This flexibility is particularly important given that children may be less skilled at expressing themselves verbally, or may not be able to understand concepts if they are not presented in a variety of ways that match learning styles and developmental levels.

Years ago, Wagner (1966, p. 28) identified specific reasons why REBT is superior to other therapeutic approaches for children:

1. REBT makes immediate direct intervention possible, when needed, to deal with school problems.
2. The basic principles can be easily understood, applied, and adapted to children of most ages and intelligence levels.
3. Rational counseling generally takes less time than other therapies, permitting more effective use of the counselor's time.
4. Rational counseling helps the child learn to live in her or his own environment.

Rational emotive behavior therapy has been employed successfully with children and adolescents for numerous problems including disruptive behavior, school phobia, fear, aggression, low self-esteem, anxiety, interpersonal relationship issues, withdrawal, impulsivity, cheating, lack of motivation, underachievement, anger, and depression (Bernard & Joyce, 1984; Wilde, 1992). While some practitioners have questioned the applicability of REBT with younger children because of their limited ability to cognitively process concepts, experience has shown that the thinking skills involved in REBT can be modified and modeled for children of any age, particularly if the practitioner is creative in adapting the approach to the child's level. In a review of significant research conducted over a decade ago, DiGiuseppe, Miller, and Trexler (1979) stated, "Studies indicate that elementary school children are capable of acquiring knowledge of rational-emotive principles and that the modification of a child's self-verbalizations or irrational self-statements can have a positive effect on emotional adjustment and behavior" (p. 225). Furthermore, because young children are in the concrete operational stage of thinking, the teachable concepts inherent in this theoretical approach offer a highly effective, concrete way of matching therapeutic style with cognitive development (Vernon, 1993b).

Perhaps the most important reason to use REBT with children and adolescents is that it gets to the "heart" of the problem; it is not just a band-aid approach to help kids temporarily feel better. As Harper (cited in Wilde, 1992) expressed, "I used to think it was enough to make kids feel better, but almost any adult can do that. I now know it is more important to teach them to think better" (p. 21). Wilde (1992) noted that REBT empowers children by "arming" them with knowledge and skills, emphasizing that this information can be utilized in present as well as future problematic situations. Teaching children how to *get* better, rather than simply *feel* better, contributes to long-lasting change and makes this therapeutic approach very effective with young clients.

PROBLEM CONCEPTUALIZATION AND THE ASSESSMENT PROCESS

There are several distinguishing features of REBT assessment with children and adolescents: (a) the relationship between the practitioner and young client; (b) the assessment of irrational beliefs; (c) parental involvement in the assessment process; (d) practical and emotional problem assessment; and (e) the developmental level of the client. In addition, the frequency, intensity, and duration of the presenting problem are important factors in problem assessment, particularly for children and adolescents.

It should be noted that assessment from an REBT perspective is ongoing, and that there is no clear distinction between assessment and intervention. In every session the therapist is constantly analyzing cognitions, emotions, and behaviors as they relate to the problem. Therefore, within the same session there may be an assessment of one aspect of a given issue and an intervention for another. Nor is it uncommon for new information to surface during an intervention which provides more assessment data.

In conceptualizing the problem, the REBT therapist can usually expect children and adolescents to first describe what is called the "Activating Event," which is what the client experienced; in other words, what happened. Unlike less directive therapists, the REBT therapist does not encourage the child to elaborate on the event, because such detail is often unnecessary. Instead, as the client presents the problem, it is important not only to listen, but to ask well-directed questions, which provide information about the client's emotional and behavioral reactions and irrational beliefs.

Establishing the Relationship

Children and adolescents generally do not refer themselves for counseling, nor do they "own" the problem or understand why they are coming to see you. Therefore, it is not at all uncommon to get a shrug of the shoulders and an "I don't know" mumbled in response to a question about what problem they would like to work on. Given this situation, it becomes more challenging, but extremely important, for the helping professional to establish a good relationship with the young client. Although Ellis does not consider a positive practitioner-client relationship to be an absolutely essential component of effective treatment (Ellis & Dryden, 1987), Bernard and Joyce (1984) stressed that with young clients, the relationship is often a necessary precondition for change. They advocate employing as many techniques as possible to establish a positive relationship. Walen, DiGiuseppe, and Wessler (1980) recommend patience, encouragement, gentle confrontation, and a slower pace when working with younger populations.

The following case illustrates relationship building and problem conceptualization with a 16-year-old adolescent male, Nathan. Nathan was referred for counseling by his parents, who were concerned about his depressed mood and anxiety about a variety of issues. Examples of interventions employed with this particular client will be subsequently described in this chapter.

Relationship building. When Nathan's father called to set up the initial appointment, the therapist talked with him briefly about his concern for Nathan. At this time, the therapist learned that Nathan, who was normally relatively outgoing and cheerful, seemed somewhat depressed, was frequently irritable and angry, and was also anxious about what his father termed "little things." Although Nathan had never been much of a risk-taker, his father noted that during the past few months he had become very concerned about what others thought, which in turn contributed to behavioral inhibitions. The therapist indicated that she preferred to see Nathan alone the first time, and learned from his father that Nathan was coming only reluctantly.

During the initial visit, Nathan appeared quite anxious and was not very verbal. In order to establish rapport, the therapist mentioned to Nathan that she knew he had been reluctant to come, and reassured him that that was all right. She asked him what it *meant* to him to come to counseling, and he immediately stated that he thought he must be crazy because he had to see a "shrink." The therapist clarified that in fact he was not crazy, but that according to his father, he had seemed less cheerful than usual and became upset more easily. She explained that this is often very common in adolescence, and noted that it can be a very difficult time for kids because there are so many changes occurring with them physically. Consequently, she said, their emotions are sometimes like a roller coaster, which makes life a little tough. She also told Nathan that she was working with lots of other kids his age, and indicated that based on what his father had said, his problems seemed like "normal" adolescent problems that she thought she could help him with.

Since Nathan appeared quite anxious about the counseling process, the therapist asked him if this explanation had helped, and whether he had any questions. She indicated that in order to work on the problem, she would need his cooperation in sharing information and feelings. She then invited Nathan to share some things about himself to help her know him better: what were his hobbies, did he play sports, was he involved in music or drama, what was his family like, what did he like to do in his free time? As he talked, Nathan seemed to relax a bit, and there was some humorous exchange as he discussed his relationship with his younger sister.

By "demystifying" the counseling process, reassuring the client that he wasn't "crazy," but did have some issues which could in all likelihood be resolved, and by being personable and relaxed, the therapist was able to establish a reasonable rapport with her client. In addition, she also treated her young client with respect. When she explained the concept of confidentiality later in the session, she did so in a straightforward manner that didn't make the process seem more of a mystery. She didn't promise that she would never tell *anyone* anything that he said, because in reality, it is often both extremely critical and desirable to consult with parents or teachers about a child's progress in therapy or issues that they should be aware of.

The therapist stated to Nathan that it might be helpful to invite his parents to join them during the latter part of the session for 10 to 15 minutes. In explaining this to Nathan, she said, "Parents often want to know what we talk about in these sessions, and I don't like to be in the middle, trying to decide what I should or shouldn't tell. Also, sometimes it is important for them to learn some new parenting techniques, or to be aware of the things that you are trying to change. So, before they come in, I will ask you if there anything we discussed that you don't want them to know about at this time. The exception to this procedure occurs if you are at risk for doing harm to yourself or others. Next, I will ask you to share something about the session with your parents . . . a goal, a homework assignment, or a concern that you would like to raise with them. In this way, we can work out any issues that might be important for everyone to deal with." This strategy demonstrates to young clients that you respect their right to confidentiality and at the same time opens communication lines with parents or involves them in the therapeutic process as needed.

In addition to what has been discussed, one of the most important relationship-building techniques is to be a good listener. Unfortunately, many practitioners have the mistaken belief that because of its active-directive nature, listening isn't essential in the practice of effective REBT. It is critical, however, particularly with children and adolescents, to be empathetic and listen without interrupting in the rapport-building stage (Bernard & Joyce, 1984; Vernon, 1983, 1989d).

The Assessment of Irrational Beliefs

According to REBT, emotional disturbance results when an individual holds irrational beliefs about an Activating Event. Identifying and disputing these irrational beliefs is the essence of REBT therapy. Irrational beliefs derive from absolute demands on self, others, and the world (Ellis, 1984; Ellis & Dryden, 1987), and are characterized by self-downing, discomfort anxiety or low frustration tolerance, awfulizing, and demandingness.

Specific aspects of problem assessment and the process of identifying irrational beliefs are illustrated with the following ongoing description of Nathan's REBT counseling.

Problem conceptualization and assessment with Nathan. After establishing rapport, the therapist invited Nathan to describe the problem as he saw it. Nathan indicated that he sometimes felt bad and that he also got angry a lot. To get a more specific picture, the therapist asked Nathan to describe what he meant when he said he felt "bad": how often he felt this way, how long each "bad" period usually lasted, and how he acted when he felt like this. She also asked him to talk more about the anger: Were there certain events that seemed to trigger it? How intense was it, how did he act when he was angry, and how long did he stay angry? With this information, the therapist was able to more accurately understand that these feelings had begun to surface more frequently during the last year, and that they seemed most prevalent when there were relationship problems with his friends or his girlfriend, or when his parents tried to control his time and his life. When questioned about school, Nathan shared that he had never been a very good student and that he felt bad when teachers criticized him or when he couldn't figure out how to do something. He also described himself as a "so-so" athlete and a good drum player.

As she listened, the therapist began to formulate some hypotheses about the cognitions contributing to Nathan's emotional and behavioral upsets. She wanted to determine whether Nathan was evaluating situations in a self-defeating way, whether he seemed to have an accurate view of reality, and whether or not he possessed appropriate self-helping cognitions (Waters, 1982). As Nathan elaborated by citing some specific examples, the therapist learned that many of his negative feelings were associated with self-downing thoughts; that he didn't see himself having many options for controlling his feelings or his behavior; and that many of his reactions were based on things that he assumed, rather than on objective facts of a given situation. Although he wasn't always adept at expressing his feelings, the therapist could usually infer the feeling based on how he described his behavior. For example, he shared that he had stormed out of the field house after the coach "chewed him out during practice." The therapist then noted that he must have been angry, and proceeded to ask him what he was thinking that resulted in the anger and the aggressive behavior. Based on his feelings and behavior, the therapist already had a hunch as to her client's operative irrational belief, because according to REBT theory, anger usually results from an other-directed abso-lutistic demand such as "The coach shouldn't chew me out during practice." Likewise, an absolutistic demand placed on oneself may contribute to depression or guilt as a result of self-downing. The REBT therapist can be reasonably sure that if the feeling is depression or guilt, rather than anger, the client is directing the "should" at himself rather than at others, and can ask appropriate questions to elicit the specific belief (e.g., "What does it say about you if you were chewed out and other players weren't?").

Verbal cues were also used to pinpoint specific irrational beliefs. Low frustration tolerance can be identified through statements such as "I don't want to change my behavior because it's too hard," while discomfort anxiety can be expressed as fear: "I'm afraid to ask the coach for help because he might think I'm a wimp."

Many times Nathan was not able to identify cognitions on his own, and the therapist had to use a variety of techniques to facilitate verbalization. Direct questioning such as the following was helpful (Bernard & Joyce, 1984, p. 195):

"What were you thinking when _____ happened?"
"What sorts of things were you saying to yourself?"
"What first comes to your mind when you think about _____ ?"

Occasionally it was necessary to use some selective labeling as a technique when Nathan had difficulty verbalizing cognitions: "When your girlfriend doesn't call you when she says she will, are you thinking that she doesn't care about the relationship?"

Even though it was often difficult to get this client to express the cognitions involved in his upsets, it was vitally important for the practitioner to assess the evaluative component of these cognitions to get to the core irrational beliefs. This was done by asking questions such as "And . . .?," "And so . . .?," "And what does that mean?" or "Because?" For example, Nathan was upset because his girlfriend had decided to spend the weekend with her friends instead of going out with him. When asked what he was thinking that made him so upset, he replied that it must mean that his girlfriend didn't like him and liked her girlfriends better. Rather than disputing the inference that his girlfriend didn't like him, the therapist assessed his appraisal of the incident by asking, "And what does it say about you if she chooses to spend time with others?"—to which Nathan replied, "I must not be good enough; there's something wrong with me." It is important to focus on the *meaning* ascribed to the inference, rather than on the inference itself, in order to elicit the irrational belief. The process is rather like peeling away layers on an onion—the more you peel, the greater the likelihood that you will be addressing the key factors which result in the emotional upset.

It is also important to ask clarifying questions to assess the specific irrational belief, as illustrated by this exchange with Nathan:

NATHAN: I can't believe that I didn't get selected for Honor Band. I am *furious.*

THERAPIST: Can you tell me more about this? When you say you are furious, what exactly is it about this situation that upsets you so much?

NATHAN: I mean that I have *never* been so mad. I just don't understand why I didn't make it after all I've done. I should have gotten in instead of the creeps that did.

THERAPIST: It sounds like you are not angry with yourself or questioning your abilities, but that you are angry with the committee who selected others instead of you.

NATHAN: Exactly.

THERAPIST: Tell me more about what you were thinking about not being selected.

NATHAN: That they are stupid and prejudiced against people who wear their hair different, and that they just picked their favorites.

THERAPIST: Suppose they did act stupidly or were prejudiced, what is it that upsets you about that?

NATHAN: That they shouldn't be that way . . . it's not fair. I might not be smart, but I know I'm the best drummer in the band. This sucks.

The "it's not fair," the demand that others should treat him the way he wants to be treated, and that they should be blamed and punished because they didn't, is the irrational belief. However, it was important for the therapist to clarify that it was a demand on others, not on self, which was upsetting him. Listening to the specific feelings—anger, as opposed to depression, in this case—helped to pinpoint the specific irrational beliefs. It was important to check this out, however, because accurate identification affects the direction the therapist takes with the counseling process.

Parental Involvement in the Assessment Process

For several reasons, it is important to involve parents in the assessment and intervention process. First of all, we can't always assume that the child is the problem, even though she or he is the identified client. Secondly, because children and adolescents don't generally refer themselves for counseling, it is oftentimes essential to have parental input about how the parents conceptualize the problem. As mentioned above, it is very common to ask young clients what problem they'd like to discuss, and to receive the response "I don't know; everything's fine." Remember that this may be their perception, or that they may be ashamed to admit that there is a problem because this would further reinforce the idea that there is something "wrong" with them. The therapist can do one of several things in this event:

1.   Share with the young client what you know about the reason for the referral and begin to teach some REBT educational concepts that relate to this issue.

2.   Deal directly with the shame issue by asking the client to share what it says about them if they are receiving counseling. This may elicit the self-downing beliefs, which can be gently disputed by reassuring them that just because they may have a problem it doesn't mean that they are a "no good" kid. This concept can be reinforced by asking clients to draw a circle and to put some plus and minus signs inside of it. They are then invited to verbalize what they see as their strengths or pluses, as well as their weaknesses, or minuses. Emphasize that all people have both strengths and weaknesses, and that the fact that they are here to work on an area of weakness doesn't mean that they are a bad person.

3.   Invite the parent(s) to attend the session and address their concerns in the presence of the child.

Although Nathan did appear to represent his problem quite accurately, his parents were consulted after the initial visit to determine whether or not they had any concerns or information which might facilitate more accurate problem assessment. At this time, the therapist learned more about the parent-adolescent conflicts and Nathan's anxiety.

Since one of the major convictions of REBT is self-help and education, parents need to be involved in the assessment and treatment process so that they can learn rational principles to employ with their children to reinforce what is occurring in therapy.

Although this was not the case with Nathan's parents, it is very common for parents themselves to have irrational beliefs which result in emotional problems and ineffective parenting. Several prominent REBT practitioners (Barrish & Barrish, 1985, 1989; Bernard & Joyce, 1984; Hauck, 1983) have identified beliefs such as the following which underlie parental anger, depression, discomfort, anxiety, fear, and guilt: "My child must always behave the way I want her/him to behave" (anger); "Unkind words, behaviors, and gestures from children can hurt us emotionally" (depression); "It is best to avoid dealing with difficult issues for as long as possible" (discomfort anxiety); "I can't help worrying about my child; worry is a sign of good parenting" (fear); "If I make a mistake it will always affect my child" (guilt).

Irrational beliefs also have a significant impact on parenting style. For instance, many parents believe that children should not be frustrated, which results in an overly permissive parenting style (Hauck, 1967). Likewise, there are parents who believe that getting angry is an effective way to modify a child's behavior, or that parents are always correct and should exercise authority in all situations, which leads to harsh and overly strict parenting (DiGiuseppe, 1981). Parents who are inconsistent in their parenting style irrationally believe that they might inconvenience themselves by being consistent, which naturally results in inconsistent parenting (Barrish & Barrish, 1989). Because problems presented by or about children and adolescents are generally so closely connected with parental emotions and behaviors, it is essential to address these issues, because working only with the child may not target the real problem.

Practical and Emotional Problem Assessment

Distinguishing between practical and emotional problems is an important aspect of REBT assessment. According to Waters (1982), practical problems are realistic difficulties which involve lack of behavioral skills for dealing with the problem, whereas emotional problems are generated by irrational beliefs and result in dysfunctional feelings. If a child has no friends, for example, the practical problem could be her lack of social skills. The emotional problem could be anxiety about initiating contact with others. If the therapist only helped the client develop new ways to meet friends, this would be a practical solution which might be helpful in terms of remediating the skill deficit. However, unless the underlying emotional problem (i.e., anxiety about initiating contacts) is resolved, the client may fail to implement her newly learned skills.

In some cases there is not an accompanying emotional problem, but it is very important to assess this and to recognize that clients very often give themselves an emotional problem about their practical problem. This concept is further illustrated below.

Addressing emotional and practical problems. Nathan had discussed how upset he got when he couldn't do something right: his homework, finding his way around a neighboring community which was larger than his own, and stocking the shelves correctly at work. Had the therapist only worked with him on developing more assertive behavior in order to ask for help, she would have been addressing the practical problem. However, the emotional problems—which included his feelings about having to ask for help and his fear of taking a risk—had to be dealt with in order for problem resolution to occur. Once Nathan was able to see that asking for help didn't mean he was dumb and stupid, he was able to practice some assertive skills and realize that he was much less anxious once he had asked for help.

As indicated by this example, practical problem-solving, which is usually behavioral in nature, addresses the symptom. The accompanying emotional problem-solving cuts to the "heart" of the issue and leads to long-lasting change.

Developmental Level

Effective assessment and intervention with children and adolescents cannot occur without taking into consideration their developmental level. There are several reasons why this is so. First of all, many children do not have the cognitive capacity to comprehend certain concepts, or they may not have the verbal ability to express thoughts and feelings in the assessment process. Bernard and Joyce (1984) cautioned that prior to age 11 when children begin to move into formal operational thinking, the disputational process in particular is difficult to grasp. They noted that it is essential to use very concrete approaches with young children so as to better match their developmental abilities.

Second, practitioners need to be aware of stages of development so they know specifically what they need to do in order to adapt assessment techniques and intervention strategies appropriately.

Third, the problem itself can be better understood by putting it in the context of what is normal at various developmental levels. For example, in working with Nathan, the therapist knew that young adolescents generally experience emotional ups and downs. She recognized that they also may tend to be very irrational because they are wavering between concrete and formal operational thinking, and that once they attain the formal thinking stage, they are more likely to see all sides of an issue and reason more effectively. Knowing what is characteristic helped the practitioner assess the problem with Nathan within the developmental context, which in turn provided a helpful perspective for the client, his parents, and the therapist.

THE INTERVENTION PROCESS

Successful problem resolution is dependent on accurate assessment as well as application of appropriate interventions. In working with children and adolescents, it is important to keep in mind that because their sense of time is so immediate, what may be a problem one week might not be a problem the next. Therefore, it is preferable that interventions target a specific aspect of the problem and be accompanied by homework assignments which reinforce concepts presented within the session. With younger clients, it is advisable to use concrete analogies, relevant examples, and interventions that relate to their personal interests. For example, if you know that 7-year-old Amelia likes to draw cartoons, an intervention to help her reduce her fears about staying overnight at a friend's house would be to have her make a cartoon book illustrating her fears and what she could think or do to chase the fears away.

Other important considerations in designing interventions for children and adolescents are discussed and illustrated below.

Adapt Techniques According to Age

Example: In working with Nathan it was apparent that he subscribed to a lot of overgeneralized thinking. He consistently read more into situations than the facts accounted for. To address this problem with an age-appropriate activity, the therapist invited Nathan to keep a record of his dysfunctional thoughts, the accompanying emotion, and a rebuttal for each irrational belief. Had Nathan been a younger child, the writing activity could have been replaced by a board game. When he landed on a particular color, he would talk about an upsetting event, and the therapist could help him identify what he might be telling himself to create the negative feeling and what he could do to change it.

Use Concrete Activities to Present and Reinforce Concepts

Example: Nathan struggled a lot with self-downing. If criticized, he frequently commented that he was dumb. When friends didn't spend time with him, he blamed himself: "If I was better at sports, they'd want to be with me. If I was better looking, my girlfriend would like me better." In working on this aspect of the problem, the therapist did several things. First of all, she had Nathan complete the *Circle of Self* activity (Vernon, 1989c), which required Nathan to describe characteristics of himself in several dimensions: physical, social, emotional, intellectual, and spiritual. In discussing this activity, the therapist helped Nathan see that he was a complex person with many dimensions. Therefore, strengths in one area could be viewed as compensating for real or perceived weaknesses in another. As a follow-up intervention, the therapist had Nathan choose an older person whom he admired, and instructed him to interview this person, asking him or her to identify their strengths *and* weaknesses in each of the dimensions identified in the previous activity. In this way, Nathan was able to see that his uncle, whom he truly looked up to, also saw himself as having weaknesses. The therapist also had Nathan do some research on his favorite drummers to learn more about their personal strengths and weaknesses.

Use Relevant Examples and Interventions

Invite young clients to share pictures and yearbooks to help you learn more about their interests, friends, and experiences. This information can then be used in several meaningful ways.

Example: After Nathan's recent music camp experience, he shared his pictures with the therapist and then proceeded to express how lonely he had been because nobody ever paid attention to him. After listening to these complaints, the therapist made this gentle observation: "Nathan, you've been telling me about how you were ignored and how miserable you were at camp, but as I look at these pictures, it appears that you are laughing and involved in several activities with others. I'm wondering if you actually didn't have some fun after all, and that perhaps you are overgeneralizing just a bit about how nobody ever paid any attention to you?" Following this, the therapist used several other relevant interventions to address Nathan's problem of "blowing things out of proportion," which usually resulted in depressed, or sometimes angry, feelings. First of all, she had him pretend that he was giving advice to his best friend about how to deal with his feelings when his friends didn't ask him out or his girlfriend didn't act like he thought she should. With coaching, the therapist was able to help Nathan verbalize to his "friend" that he needed to check out the facts before he jumped to conclusions. She also had him bring in examples of popular songs which he thought represented sensible and nonsensible ways of thinking.

Don't "Skim the Surface" with Behavioral Interventions

Sometimes, clients whom you think are too young or inexperienced to learn disputational techniques or understand the cognitive components may in fact benefit from them.

Example: Nathan repeatedly became upset when his parents asked him to do something that he thought he shouldn't have to do. Behaviorally, the therapist could have suggested that if he didn't like the consequence of being grounded, he should practice being more cooperative. Instead, she helped Nathan and his parents understand why this was becoming such an issue. She first drew from her knowledge of developmental theory and explained to the parents that some of Nathan's resistance might be due to the fact that as an adolescent, he is at the stage where he is trying to become independent and make his own decisions. Therefore, when they require him to do something immediately, he may interpret this as their not trusting him to make his own decisions and, in essence, thwarting his attempts at independence. With Nathan, she explained the difference between demanding and preferring, noting that his anger was related to his belief that his parents *should not* tell him what to do and that he *should* be able to determine what he did with his time. She then showed him how to change that thinking by asking him if he really thought that he should *never* have to do *anything* he didn't want to do, or if this was simply the way he would *prefer* it. She pointed out that he would be less angry if he gave up his demands not to do things he didn't want to do, and asked him if, in reality, teenagers usually did have to do some things they didn't particularly like to do. Once Nathan understood the distinction between demands and preferences, he was able to apply it to other situations as well.

Take Cues from the Client

If you see too many blank stares or hear yourself asking too many questions which are answered with an "I don't know," try varying your approach. Consider using props, drawings, music, mutual storytelling, games, role-playing, or other age-appropriate strategies to involve the child or adolescent in the process.

Example: After meeting with some resistance in trying to dispute Nathan's anger-generating irrational beliefs, specifically, that his mother *should* treat him exactly like he wanted to be treated all the time, the therapist suggested that maybe Nathan enjoyed the anger, and encouraged him to make a list of all the positive outcomes of the hostile behavior that occurred as a result of his demandingness. After Nathan completed this task, the therapist suggested that he make a poster announcing "help" sessions for his friends so that they could also learn more hostile behavior which had "positive" outcomes, such as being grounded, not being able to have friends over, and losing the privilege of driving the car. By combining humor and exaggeration to match Nathan's overgeneralized, demanding irrational beliefs, the therapist was able to help him recognize that the behavior wasn't helping him, and then could deal more effectively with disputations concerning fairness.

The interventions described above were effective in helping Nathan to deal with his self-downing, his anger, and his tendency to overgeneralize and assume, which resulted in his depressed feelings. By working very concretely and teaching him specific disputational strategies, coupled with homework assignments, the therapist was able to help Nathan to "help himself" after five or six sessions. At that point, visits became more infrequent, and Nathan was given self-help forms to complete between sessions so that he could become more adept at recognizing irrational beliefs, identifying feelings, and developing more effective disputes to counteract the irrational thinking.

ANGER AND ANXIETY: TYPICAL ISSUES WITH YOUNG CLIENTS

The following pages describe specific interventions for dealing with anger and anxiety, two typical problems frequently presented by children and adolescents. Brief case examples will illustrate concepts.

Anger

If you've worked much with adolescents, you know that for many, anger is as familiar as talking on the telephone. And although this emotion is generally not as prevalent in younger children, there are situational factors which may precipitate anger for them. Because anger often results in self-defeating behaviors with significant negative consequences, it is important to help young clients understand where their anger comes from and how to deal with it effectively.

Using concrete concepts is very essential in explaining aspects of anger, and it is particularly useful in differentiating degrees of intensity of this emotion. A simple strategy is to use masking tape to make a continuum on the floor. As young clients discuss their anger about a particular incident, explain that there is a difference between being *irritated,* or a *little bit angry,* versus being *very angry,* as in *rage.* Invite them to stand on the line which identifies exactly how angry they are. This is a very good way to clarify the exact nature of their anger and to confront discrepancies between their behavior and how angry they profess to be. Consequently, this can lead to a simple explanation of behaviors and beliefs that correspond to the intensity of their anger, as illustrated in the following example.

Ten-year-old Peter had been getting in trouble at school because he would throw a tantrum and rip up his papers when they were returned with a bad grade. When asked to take a position on the anger continuum, Peter stood closer to the irritation end. The therapist said, "Peter, I notice that you aren't standing close to the 'very angry' point, and yet as you describe how you act when you get your papers back, it looks as if you are very angry. If you were just irritated, you might feel a little upset and you might be thinking that it's frustrating to keep trying and still get papers back with bad grades. But, because you are throwing a tantrum, you are probably thinking that it's awful that you are getting bad grades all the time and that the teacher probably isn't being fair. Or, you could be mad at yourself and think that you are dumb and stupid because you keep getting bad grades. So, do you see how there is a real connection between how you feel and what you think and do?" Following this explanation, the therapist encouraged Peter to share more about what he was thinking, which clarified the irrational beliefs which needed to be challenged in order to reduce the intensity of the anger.

Other suggestions for dealing with anger in young clients are described below.

Ask clients to identify ways anger helps them achieve their goals. Example: Seventeen-year-old Shalanda was constantly being sent to detention and threatened with expulsion because of her defiant behavior at school. Disputing her irrational beliefs about how unfair her teachers were wasn't working, so the therapist shifted the focus to "How is what you're doing helping you achieve your goal, which is to graduate and get away from these 'awful' teachers?" Even though she was reluctant to let go of her anger, this strategy helped Shalanda realize that her behavior wasn't helping her achieve her goal, and she was willing to establish a behavioral plan to stop the defiance.

Help clients look at the payoffs of anger. Angry children and adolescents often feel rather self-righteous about their anger, and they are reluctant to give it up because it helps them feel powerful. Because of this, disputation is often ineffective, and the anger initially has to be dealt with more inelegantly by having them focus on the positive and negative payoffs of the anger. Although this strategy is similar to looking at anger in relation to goal attainment, this technique is more appropriate for younger children, since younger children may not clearly understand the concept of goal attainment, which is often more long-term in nature.

An example of helping clients look at payoffs is as follows: Kevin and his brother were frequently engaged in name-calling, yelling, and physical fights. Both insisted that their feelings, thoughts, and behaviors were very justified. While neither seemed willing to stop the behavior, they didn't like the consequence, which was being grounded. In working with these boys, the therapist asked them to list the positive and negative payoffs of the anger. Since there were more negatives than positives, the therapist was able to concretely point out that the anger and expression of it appeared to be doing more harm than good, and at this point was able to obtain a reluctant acknowledgment that it might be good to look at ways to reduce the anger or express it differently. To teach these concepts, the therapist used the book *The Mouse, the Monster, and Me* (Palmer, 1977), which explains the difference between assertive, aggressive, and nonassertive behavior by using the concrete images of the mouse (nonassertive), the monster (aggressive), and the "me" (assertive). The boys readily identified with the descriptions of the behaviors associated with each type, and learned how to reduce demands to preferences so they could behave more assertively.

Introduce the "instant replay" concept. Bedford's (1974) book, *Instant Replay,* is an excellent way to help younger children stop and assess their behavior and deal with the thoughts that created the anger and aggression. After reading the book, engage children in role-playing what occurred between the characters in the book when they were angry. Next, discuss what the children were telling themselves about this situation, and ways in which they could change this thinking so that they wouldn't react so angrily. The book serves as a concrete means of introducing content, and the concept of "instant replay" can be used as a homework assignment: "Next time you feel yourself getting angry, think about the instant replay. Stop your action, think about what is making you upset, say different things to yourself, and redirect your anger."

Anxiety

Anxiety is not an uncommon emotion for children and adolescents, in part because their level of comprehension about events may be limited, or because they naturally extrapolate ideas from one context and inappropriately apply them to another situation which is totally different. As an example, a father once called the school counselor and was concerned because his 8-year-old son was suddenly anxious about going to sleep at night and had written a will, giving his possessions away. The father was in a panic and wanted the counselor to meet with his son to see what was wrong. In talking with John, the counselor learned that the class had been discussing current events, in particular the bombings of some villages in Somalia where a number of children had been killed. John told the counselor that he made his will because he wanted to leave some of his favorite things to his cousins in case someone bombed his house or school. In this case, John didn't have enough facts to differentiate the possibility of something like this happening from the probability of it occurring, and therefore was very anxious. Once the counselor was able to help him see that things like that were unlikely to occur in their small Midwestern community, the anxiety disappeared.

As this situation illustrates, it is important for adults to understand how children's cognitive abilities may interfere with their ability to correctly process information. Because of this, it is critical to try and anticipate how the child may interpret situations and offer explanations to prevent the anxiety.

Two examples of cases which identify specific interventions for dealing with anxiety follow. The first pertains to a young child, and the second to an adolescent.

The case of 8-year-old Jennifer. Jennifer's parents brought her to therapy because of her anxiety about bad things happening to the family. Her problem had begun a year before when they were staying in a hotel where the fire alarm went off during the night. Although it was a minor fire and no one was injured, Jennifer continued to be worried. Later in the summer, she was staying with her elderly grandmother and a tornado touched down nearby. According to Jennifer, she and her grandmother had gone to a storm cellar, but when they tried to get out they were not strong enough to push the door open and were trapped for a short while. In addition to these concerns, she was worried about being in a car accident.

Jennifer was a very verbal child, and it was not difficult for her to describe her fear. To get a specific assessment of the intensity of her anxiety and the frequency with which it occurred, the therapist gave her three charts marked with the days of the week. For each worry, she was to mark a 1–10 (low to high) each day. During the next visit, they discussed Jennifer's degree of worry, which was higher for the accidents because they were in a car daily, and for the storms because the weather had been changeable. To determine the specific thoughts about each of these fears, the therapist asked this young client to make a list of the things she thought about in relation to each. For storms, Jennifer listed the following: A tornado would destroy their home, bad lightning would set their house on fire, or high winds would knock trees into their house. For the car accident, Jennifer listed herself and family members being seriously hurt, or one or more of them dying in a crash.

To deal with the anxiety about the weather, the therapist gave Jennifer a chart and asked her to watch the weather portion of the news each night. She was supposed to note the following based on her observations: Was the following day going to be (a) sunny and pleasant; (b) cloudy, but no rain; (c) rainy, but no storms; (d) windy and rainy; (e) high winds, rain, lightning, and thunder; or (f) tornado. When she and the therapist discussed the information, Jennifer was able to see that there had been no bad storms all week. To see if this was more of an exception than a rule, Jennifer charted the weather for several weeks to help her see that there had been severe weather only very occasionally. She and the therapist also researched tornadoes in the encyclopedia, discussing the rare combinations of circumstances needed to produce them. She learned to use self-talk (The weather is not horribly bad very often; instead of being upset all the time, I can learn what to do in case of a tornado; I can keep reminding myself that a bad storm does not mean there will be a tornado; the worst thing that could happen is that our house will be destroyed and we will die, and this has never happened in my town) to reinforce the idea that although bad things can happen, it is not necessary to worry every day. To deal with the other two concerns, the therapist used a similar strategy. She had Jennifer interview her father, an insurance salesman, about the number of serious car accidents compared with more minor ones; read the newspaper to chart occurrences of fires; and interview the fire chief. Self-talk was generated for these two situations as well.

Over time, with the use of the concrete strategies and self-talk, Jennifer was able to reduce her level of anxiety.

The case of 13-year-old Marcus. Marcus' parents initiated therapy because he had recently started skipping school as a seventh grader. Because Marcus was extremely shy and resisted talking about his school attendance problem, the therapist asked him to write responses to several unfinished sentences so that he could understand what was causing the anxiety at school. Examination of Marcus's responses suggested that he was more concerned about being made fun of in the locker room than he was about academics. The therapist learned that this was the first year that students had to dress for physical education. Because he was slight and immature, the therapist hypothesized that Marcus was not as fully developed as his peers, which could result in the teasing that he had expressed concern about on the unfinished sentence activity. Furthermore, his responses indicated he was afraid of getting bad grades in school because junior high seemed a lot harder than elementary school; also, because the routine was confusing, he was anxious about getting to the right class on time.

To address these problems, the therapist first assured Marcus that these concerns were typical for his age and that a lot of his friends were probably experiencing the same anxiety. Second, he adapted an activity called "Magnify" (Pincus, 1990), in which several events were listed and Marcus was instructed to magnify their importance by turning them into a catastrophe. For example:

1. You walk into class late because you could not get your locker open. Catastrophic thought: _____
2. You go into the locker room to change for physical education. Catastrophic thought: _____
3. You do not understand how to do an assignment. Catastrophic thought: _____
4. Someone teases you in the locker room. Catastrophic thought: _____

After Marcus identified the worst-case scenario, the therapist taught him to look at the probable situation by adapting "Getting Straight Our Magnifications" (Pincus, 1990). Example:

You walk into class late because you could not get your locker open: Best case scenario: _____

Worst case scenario (previous activity): _____
Probable scenario: _____

By identifying best, worst, and probable outcomes for each question, Marcus began to dispute some of his anxieties about various seventh-grade issues. The therapist also helped him look at best and worst case scenarios for not going to school, and then helped him develop self-statements such as the following to deal with the anxiety: (a) Even though it seems like everyone is looking at me, they probably all aren't; (b) Even if everyone is looking at me, it doesn't mean that there is something wrong with me; (c) If I don't understand an assignment, I can ask the teacher and it doesn't mean I'm dumb.

By working with him in this way, the therapist eventually helped Marcus see that even if he was somewhat uncomfortable in junior high, he could stand the discomfort. By looking at the worst-case scenario, he was able to put the problem in better perspective and not "awfulize," as is characteristic of young adolescents.

CONCLUSION

The purpose of this chapter has been to promote application of rational emotive behavior therapy with children and adolescents. As emphasized throughout the chapter, this therapeutic approach has been used successfully to help children and adolescents learn to deal with problems in constructive ways. Because rational emotive behavior therapy embraces a wide variety of cognitive, emotive, and behavioral techniques, the therapist has great flexibility in adapting concepts to match specific client needs. As previously emphasized, the intent of REBT is to help children *get* better, not just *feel* better. The skills that are taught to young clients can serve them throughout their lives to prevent or minimize both situationally specific and developmentally related problems.

As an adolescent recently remarked, "I used to be so angry and I didn't know why. I kept thinking that the only way things could be better would be if my mother changed. Now I know that she'll probably stay like she is, but I don't have to get so mad. I can change my thoughts so that I won't get so upset, mouth off, and get grounded."

Rational emotive behavior therapy empowers children and adolescents to "take charge" of their lives in order to be happier and more productive. As we hear repeatedly, children are our hope for the future. It behooves us to do all we can to assure their healthy development. Using rational emotive behavior therapy is a good way to facilitate this goal.

REFERENCES

Barrish, H. H., & Barrish, I. J. (1985). *Managing parental anger.* Shawnee Mission, KS: Overland Press.

Barrish, I. J., & Barrish, H. H. (1989). *Surviving and enjoying your adolescent.* Kansas City, MO: Westport.

Bedford, S. (1974). *Instant replay.* New York: Institute for Rational Living.

Bernard, M., & Joyce, M. (1984). *Rational-emotive therapy with children and adolescents.* New York: John Wiley.

DiGiuseppe, R. A. (1975). The use of behavioral modification to establish rational self-statements in children. *Rational Living, 10,* 18–20.

DiGiuseppe, R. A. (1981). Cognitive therapy in children. In G. Emery, S. D. Hollon, & R. C. Bedrosian (Eds.), *New directions in cognitive therapy* (pp. 120–143). New York: Guilford.

DiGiuseppe, R. A., Miller, N. J., & Trexler, L. D. (1979). A review of rational-emotive psychotherapy outcome studies. In A. Ellis & J. M. Whitely (Eds.), *Theoretical and empirical foundations of rational-emotive therapy* (pp. 218–235). Monterey, CA: Brooks/Cole.

Ellis, A. (1984). The essence of RET–1984. *Journal of Rational Emotive Therapy, 2,* 19–25.

Ellis, A., & Bernard, M. E. (Eds.) (1983). *Rational-emotive approaches to the problems of childhood.* New York: Plenum.

Ellis, A., & Dryden, W. (1987). *The practice of rational-emotive therapy.* New York: Springer Publishing Company.

Ellis, A., Moseley, S., & Wolfe, J. (1966). *How to raise an emotionally healthy, happy child.* Hollywood, CA: Wilshire Books.

Hauck, P. A. (1967). *The rational management of children.* New York: Libra.

Hauck, P. A. (1983). Working with parents. In A. Ellis & M. E. Bernard (Eds.), *Rational-emotive approaches to the problems of childhood* (pp. 333–365). New York: Plenum.

Knaus, W. J. (1974). *Rational-emotive education: A manual for elementary school teachers.* New York: Institute for Rational-Emotive Therapy.

Palmer, P. (1977). *The mouse, the monster, and me.* San Luis Obispo, CA: Impact Publishers.

Pincus, D. (1990). *Feeling good about yourself: Strategies to guide young people toward more positive, personal feelings.* Carthage, IL: Good Apple.

Vernon, A. (1983). Rational-emotive education. In A. Ellis and M. E. Bernard (Eds.), *Rational-emotive approaches to the problems of childhood* (pp. 467–483). New York: Plenum.

Vernon, A. (1989a). *Help yourself to a healthier you.* Minneapolis, MN: Burgess.

Vernon, A. (1989b). *Thinking, feeling, behaving: An emotional education curriculum for children.* Champaign, IL: Research Press.

Vernon, A. (1989c). *Thinking, feeling, behaving: An emotional education curriculum for adolescents.* Champaign, IL: Research Press.

Vernon, A. (1989d). Assessment and treatment of childhood problems: Applications of rational-emotive therapy. *Counseling and Human Development, 22,* 2–11.

Vernon, A. (1993a). *Counseling children and adolescents.* Denver, CO: Love.

Vernon, A. (1993b). *Developmental assessment and intervention with children and adolescents.* Alexandria, VA: American Counseling Association.

Wagner, E. E. (1966). Counseling children. *Rational Living, 1,* 26–28.

Walen, S. R., DiGiuseppe, R. A., & Wessler, R. L. (1980). *A practitioner's guide to rational-emotive therapy.* New York: Oxford University Press.

Waters, V. (1979). *Color us rational.* New York: Institute for Rational Living.

Waters, V. (1980). *Rational stories for children.* New York: Institute for Rational-Emotive Therapy.

Waters, V. (1982). Therapies for children: Rational-emotive therapy. In C. R. Reynolds & T. B. Gutkin (Eds.), *Handbook of school psychology* (pp. 37–57). New York: John Wiley.

Wilde, J. (1992). *Rational counseling with school-aged populations: A practical guide.* Muncie, IN: Accelerated Development.

Wittmer, J. (1993). *Managing your school counseling program: K–12 developmental strategies.* Minneapolis, MN: Educational Media Corporation.

CHAPTER 3

"Shoya Moya Ik Baraba": Using REBT with Culturally Diverse Clients

**Mitchell W. Robin and
Raymond DiGiuseppe**

The appropriateness of applying the psychological theories and psychological interventions proposed by Western trained therapists to non-Western people has been questioned since the 1920s. Freud (1912/1938, 1930/1962), in his seminal writings on both the human condition and the nature and etiology of emotional disturbance, made widely reported claims for the universality of his postulates and psychosexual stages. Malinowski (1927), however, asserted that the Trobriand Islanders, for example, did not suffer from the Oedipal Complex since they did not live with their fathers and hence did not have to compete with him for their mothers' love.

We in the mental health profession that have followed in Freud's wake—whether we endorse his position or not—are still trying to respond to more current and contemporary charges that Western ideas and techniques are largely inappropriate, not only for non-Western peoples, but also for people who are from the therapist's own culture but might differ from the therapist because of religious affiliation, race, gender, sexual orientation, and/or extent of physical challenge (Simola, 1992). In the past decade a spate of articles and books has been written about cross-cultural counseling and therapy (Atkinson, Morten, & Sue, 1989; Christensen, 1989; Landrine, 1992; Pedersen, 1985; Sue & Sue, 1990; and others).[1] The general import of most of these writings has been that mental health practitioners would be well advised to intervene only in the lives of people who are culturally similar to themselves, because when they attempt to intervene in the lives of people who are culturally dissimilar they often do a less than adequate job, either because of faulty diagnosis, inherent prejudice, or lack of cultural awareness and sensitivity.

Hollingshead and Redlich (1958) made the same statement, more than 35 years ago, and pointed out that people who are of lower SES are both more likely to be wrongly diagnosed as schizophrenic and to receive little more than custodial care compared to higher-SES clients. Phyllis Chessler (1972), writing from a feminist perspective, contended that most male therapists, and many female therapists as well, were apt to misdiagnose their female clients because of their inherent male bias which predisposed them to define wellness in terms of maleness. Chessler's remarkable discovery sensitized the profession to the notion that many practitioners, at the time of publication of her book, believed that a healthy MAN was a healthy PERSON, whereas a healthy woman was a disturbed person.

The sensitivity gap is being admirably filled by the books and articles mentioned above, and countless others are sure to follow. In fact,

---

[1] It was interesting to discover that most of the articles on cross-cultural issues in psychotherapy have been published in the last 5 years. A search using the descriptors of cross-cultural differences and psychotherapy, Rational-Emotive Therapy, cognitive therapy, or cognitive psychotherapy, conducted using Psych-Lit shows that there were 163 articles published on this topic between the years 1974 and 1995. Eighty of the articles were published during the last 5 years. A more provoking discovery for REBT practitioners was that only five of those articles were based on Rational-Emotive Behavior Therapy, cognitive therapy, or cognitive psychotherapy, and all of those were published during the last 5 years. This is something which obviously needs to be rectified and which obviously is also beyond the scope of this chapter.

training in "sensitivity" seems to be one of the hallmarks of the culturally skilled counselor (Sue et al., 1981.)

In later writings Sue & Zane (1987) rethought this common admonition for cultural sensitivity and concluded it had not been helpful, because it did not fully address the process by which the therapist might integrate "sensitivity" into daily practice. More telling was their own admission that much of the literature failed to provide useful treatment procedures and ignored within group heterogeneity. They suggested that anthropological awareness should be be tied to the variables of credibility and giving. The therapist needed to be perceived both as a credible and appropriate source of care or intervention and as a "giving person". These latter variables were tested and demonstrated to be clinically useful by Lefley (1989).

THE CHALLENGE OF
CROSS-CULTURAL THERAPY

Doing therapy with culturally diverse clients is a challenge to both the therapist and the client. It provides a challenge to the therapist who may need to confront some of her cherished assumptions about what constitutes mental health, mental illness, and effective therapeutic practice. It provides a challenge to the client to see the culturally diverse practitioner as someone who can offer appropriate and effective interventions.

If therapists are to meet the challenge of doing cross-cultural therapy we need to shift from an Us *vs* Them orientation to an Us *and* Them orientation.

Us *vs.* Them

We contend that, at best, the sources cited above provide the reader with an anthropological awareness of the assumptions about the world, lifestyles, values, and customs of people who are culturally dissimilar from the majority culture. In other words, they show us (mental health professionals) how we are different from them (our culturally diverse clients). We contend that this approach serves to reinforce our clients' "otherness." These sources remind the mental health professional that people who are culturally different have different expectations about the healing process; different assumptions about what issues need to be addressed, and different definitions of successful outcome. At worst, they remove hope: both the therapist's hope that she can provide useful and timely interventions for her clients regardless of background, and the client's hope that she can be helped when confronted with a therapist who is culturally dissimilar.

This latter criticism is not presented lightly. In an ever-widening multi-cultural environment it is a rare practitioner who is not confronted, at least occasionally, with a client who comes from a different background than herself. It is a common experience, at least in the United States of America, for minority group clients (and this can be construed to mean numbers of racial, religious, and sexual minority groups, as well as people with disabilities) to be treated by culturally dissimilar therapists.

In an ideal world, perhaps, everyone who needs help would be treated by someone like themselves. Currently the situation is such that minority group clients tend to be treated by practitioners who are from the majority culture. How well these clients fare will in part be determined by the skills of the therapist, the therapeutic alliance forged between the client and the therapist, and the willingness of the minority group client to see the therapist as a provider of relevant or useful skills and insights.

We contend that when respected writers tell minority clients that they can only expect prejudicial or culturally biased treatment from the hands of most of the therapists currently available, it may serve to keep even greater numbers of minority clients from seeking help in a timely fashion, and does nothing to enhance the therapeutic coping skills of the therapist who may come from a culture that is different from his/her client.

It is possible that the reason many Western-based interventions are viewed as inappropriate by non-Western clients is that these interventions are still for the most part based on a psychodynamic theory of psychotherapy. This view essentially negates the unique cultural experience of the client and attempts to homogenize all clients so that they fit the theory of the therapist. For purposes of discussion we will refer to such therapies as *content* therapies.

Content therapies essentially require that the therapist listen for specific content/context-laden cues and then respond to the implicit content of the patient's statements. This approach arguably requires that the therapist impose a structure, often her own, on the chaotic flow of the patient's ideas, and maintain the therapeutic process until the patient achieves a level of insight acceptable to the therapist (Sue & Sue, 1990).

An alternative approach would be to engage in what we will call *process* therapy. This form of therapy focuses on the change relationship itself, and imposes little or no context/content requirements other than logical consistency and factual, or where appropriate, cultural reality.[2]

Us and Them

We maintain that cognitive behavioral therapies such as those developed by Ellis (1977, 1989, 1991) and Beck (1976, 1983) are currently the most appropriate forms of therapy for use with culturally diverse clients. In particular, we argue that these forms of therapy (DiGiuseppe, Robin, & Dryden, 1990; Robin & DiGiuseppe, 1995) :

Have the least amount of extra-theoretical and extra-cultural assumptions. Cognitive therapy maintains that an individual's emotions and behaviors are largely determined by his/her cognitions. In order to help the client the therapist must therefore (1) identify those cognitions which lead to dysfunctional behaviors and emotions, (2) teach the client to develop more effective, i.e., functional, cognitions, and (3) encourage the client to integrate these newer, more effective cognitions into daily life. In order to do this the therapist need not maintain any scientifically untested or untestable hypothesis, nor does the therapist need to "believe in" a world or a world view that existed a century ago. We argue that other, i.e., noncognitive, therapies may require the client to not only "believe in" a Victorian world and world view, but also to be willing to believe in libido, cathexis, and other untestable notions.

Are tied to a visible and acceptable philosophical base—stoicism and empiricism. While it can be asserted that all contemporary Western science is based on an outgrowth of philosophical reasoning, we argue that

---

[2] For a fuller discussion of content vs. process therapies see Robin and DiGiuseppe (1995).

many current psychotherapists are not instructed in the philosophical underpinnings of their particular discipline, and as a result are not equipped to respond to a client's challenges about why specific interventions are used or recommended. Cognitive therapy, in general, and REBT, in particular, make the point of training their practitioners to know the philosophical assumptions which underlie their "science" and to use this philosophical base in their daily practice. We are therefore equipped to show the client both why and how we operate as we do.

When we intervene from the stoic's position of tolerance and acceptance we are not just using a philosophy unique to those of us from Western European culture, we are using a philosophy whose elements can be found in Native American, Eastern, and Asian cultures as well. (A brief discussion of how we might work with a client who comes from a more hedonistic philosophical tradition will be presented below).

Empiricism, while it may be a cornerstone of Western science and tradition, is not as integral a part of non-Western culture. This difference, while profound, need not be daunting. Just because REBTers are empiricists does not mean our clients *must* be. The REBT therapist is encouraged to show the client the behavioral and emotional consequences of various philosophies. While we will point out why we prefer looking for empirical proof and why we use empirical proof to support our conclusions, we will not force our clients to become empiricists. Instead, we will show them the B–C connection and how their philosophy or world view relates to their current emotional and behavioral difficulties. Once this is done, the choice is up to the client to either accept or reject the empirical B–C connection (as it pertains to his or her emotions). By actively and visibly presenting the philosophical context of our intervention, we show the client the reasoning behind our intervention and then let the client proceed from there. It has been our experience that many clients whose cultures have a nonempirical, i.e., spiritual, belief system are still willing to accept empirical proof when it is offered to them—especially when the empirical proof presented is their own improved functioning.

Are proactive, short-term and goal-directed. Many clients from culturally diverse populations expect that when they go for help they will be actively helped, that the help will be visibly focused on the presenting problem, and that the help will not require years of delay before it becomes effective (Sue & Sue, 1990; Sue & Zane, 1987). Both traditional psychoanalytic therapy and nondirective psychotherapy appear to violate these expectations. Psychoanalysts and nondirective therapists, for example, may often appear to be indifferent to clients' direct questions about presenting problems and interventions. On the other hand rational-emotive and other cognitive-behavioral therapists tend to answer direct questions with direct answers.

On the surface, both psychoanalysis and nondirective therapy appear to miss the boat as far as being directed towards the client's goals. In the case of psychoanalysis, the chief goal of therapy is for the client to develop insight as defined by the therapist. Nondirective therapy, while it is client-centered, may not meet the goal-directed criterion because clients are not directly given or taught to use the tools they need to achieve their goals.

Encourage the client to maintain his/her cultural reality and provide a basis for examining and challenging long-cherished cultural assumptions only when they lead to dysfunctional emotions and behaviors. We argue that REBT and other cognitive therapies, because of the previously stated conditions, are better suited generally to helping culturally diverse clients maintain their own cultures. The client need not abandon any deeply held convictions, nor learn to endorse beliefs that are not compatible with his/her tradition. The client is encouraged to examine the emotional and behavioral consequences of his/her endorsement of any belief system—cultural, religious, or personal. The client then has the choice of either reappraising the usefulness of specific endorsements and possibly changing his/her beliefs, or maintaining his/her long-cherished beliefs and living with the positive or negative consequences.

Provide the client with the tools to comprehend the links between beliefs, emotions, and behaviors but do not force the client to think, feel, or behave "like we do" in order to get better. This is accomplished in a number of ways: (1) by didactically providing the client with the tools for personally discovering the B–C connection, (2) by helping the client to examine the potential positive/negative consequences of any decision to change via the use of a decision tree, and (3) by showing the client that mental health, in his/her own community, is typically based on rational, i.e., logical and empirical thinking.

Are "value-free" therapies, in as much as they help the client work towards achieving his/her own personal goals within his/her own sociocultural context. The goals of cognitive therapy generally, and REBT in particular, are arrived at within the context of the therapeutic alliance; i.e, the therapist and the client agree about the problem, the potential solution, and the method to be used before therapy actively begins. These goals are personally endorsed by the client, typically because they either are the client's own specific goals, or they directly reflect the client's goals.

Enable the client to recognize when these goals are incompatible. There may be times when subcultural appropriateness is inconsistent with the dominant culture's concept of appropriateness. These areas of potential incompatibility include, but are not limited to, polygamy and health and hygiene practices. Additionally, the goal of REBT is to help the client achieve his/her goals, insofar as those goals are not legally prohibited by the dominant culture. I (M.W.R.) once worked with a client who came from a community which actively endorsed activities which would be considered spousal abuse in this culture. The husband's "job" was to physically "correct" his wife with corporal punishment whenever she erred from the straight and narrow. He was reminded that these activities were prohibited in the United States, and that if he engaged in them he might be subject to arrest. It was pointed out that while he never had to change his belief about the appropriateness of corporal punishment, if he wished to avoid unpleasant interactions with the police he would be well advised to change his behavior. While I have many strongly held personal convictions about the inappropriateness of corporal punishment for wifely indiscretions, I refrained from blaming, shaming, or labeling the client in an Us vs Them way.

Teach clients how to "think straight" about their potential incompatibility. Whether the incompatibility is as serious as the case mentioned above or is more benign, the client's discovery of this incompatibility typically provides the client with a negative A and concomitant potentially dysfunctional Cs. This provides another opportunity for the therapist to instruct the client in the B–C connection and to show how rational thinking allows for more functional, although still negative, emotional and behavioral consequences.

The above assertions are supported by the authors' experiences in training therapists in a wide variety of cultural milieus, as well as their own (Robin, DiGiuseppe, & Alvarez, 1991a, 1991b; Robin, DiGiuseppe, & Kopec, 1993a, 1993b). Repeatedly, we have heard our trainees state that REBT's approach, as described in our training sessions, was highly compatible with their own cultures, and indeed in many cases included elements which they had previously thought were unique to their particular culture. We have, for example, encountered almost universal agreement when we present REBT's view that absolutistic demands for fairness are irrational, and lead to dysfunctional consequences.

REBT reminds people that the world is not fair, even though many would prefer it to be so. REBT therapists help their clients to see that to demand that the world be different than it is does not change the world but does change one's emotions from functional to dysfunctional. Trainees from South America, Northern Europe, and Asian communities have all remarked, at different times, that they thought they were the only ones who had recognized this irrationality. In fact, many expressed surprise that people from the United States could endorse fairness as a preference rather than as a childish demand.

The senior author, during another workshop, was presenting the criteria for recognizing the difference between rational and irrational beliefs and had described the following scenario: "Your best friend has just walked by you. When he looks your way, he frowns and then walks on. What is the most rational way to describe this encounter?" Many workshop participants engaged in mindreading and pronounced that their friend was angry at them. I then pointed out that the only empirically valid, and therefore rational description, was: "My friend appeared to be frowning when he walked by me." I then showed how their mindreading might lead them to act appropriately in terms of their thoughts but potentially inappropriately to the empirical reality of the situation.

At this point one participant said, "I dreamt that . . ." I asked what she was referring to and the participant replied that she was a practitioner of Zen who had just returned from a Zen retreat in which she was given the suggestion to use the phrase "I dreamt that . . ." rather than, "I know . . ." or, "I believe . . ." The point of this exercise was to remind people that "knowledge" may be as illusory and as ephemeral as dreams, and that people would be well advised not to claim knowledge with such certainty, since the assertion of certainty can lead to undesirable consequences. She expressed delight in seeing the similarity of REBT theory to her Zen practice.

On the surface, Zen and REBT appear as compatible as fine wine and salt. Zen, while it is stoic in its outlook, appears to be the epitome of non-Western, nonempirical thought. I have worked with many clients who were Zen practitioners, and some areas of apparent commonality emerge. REBT and Zen practice both: (1) see the linkage between thoughts and feelings, (2) help people to be more accepting of what is, and (3) help people see the uselessness of demands as compared to preferences.

While REBT can, and does, work quite effectively as it is "right out of the box," two modifications in establishing the therapeutic alliance are recommended when working with culturally diverse clients. The therapeutic alliance typically requires the client and the therapist to agree on the problem being worked on, the goals for the therapy, and the language/metaphors being used. Based on our experience, we would advise that prior to attempting to establish the therapeutic goals the therapist should (1) gather data about the client's expectations about the therapeutic process, and (2) educate the client about the therapist's expectations about the therapeutic process (Robin, 1992).

Differences in therapist/client expectations have been documented to have a negative impact on the effectiveness of the cross-cultural counseling process (Boyer, 1983; Cherbosque, 1987; Deane, 1992; Jilek, 1986). In fact, in one study Cherbosque (1987) showed that counselor self-disclosure, which is sometimes viewed as a highly appropriate part of the therapeutic process, was more negatively viewed by Mexican-Americans than by Americans in general. The Mexican-Americans sampled preferred a more "formal" interaction with their counselors, and tended to rate nondisclosers as more "trustworthy" than disclosers.

These differences in expectation about disclosure once led to a rather frustrating encounter between a therapist I (M.W.R.) was supervising and a client of Hispanic origin. The client "refused to make eye contact," and my supervisee assumed that the client was either depressed and/or evasive. These assumptions on the part of the supervisee led her to develop hypotheses about the underlying irrational beliefs that the client might have been holding. When she shared her hypotheses with her client, the client informed her that she was neither depressed nor evasive. The client reminded her that they were newly acquainted and that self-disclosure between new acquaintances is of necessity limited and "guarded." The client further informed her that making eye contact with an expert was impolite and would be seen as a hostile challenge. Had my supervisee not been trained in REBT, she might not have shared her working hypotheses so openly, or she might have been tempted to dismiss the client's rejection of her hypotheses as resistance. As her supervisor, I instructed her to spend some time in (1) gathering information about the client's expectations about therapy and "normal" human interactions, and (2) educating the client about some of her own expectations about how therapy is conducted. This required that the supervisee (1) be willing to admit ignorance and, (2) tolerate the discomfort of "wasting time" spent in gathering this type of data.

USING REBT WITH CULTURALLY DIVERSE CLIENTS

Doing good cross-cultural therapy is doing good REBT.[3] The therapist uses both the Socratic approach and the hypothesis-testing skills that she has been trained to use with all her clients, but remains aware of the differences in underlying realities between herself and her client. These differences may typically reflect themselves in the client's perceptions of their own cultural uniqueness as compared to that of the therapist. A sensitive therapist, REBT or otherwise, needs to address the issue of cultural uniqueness as it makes itself felt during the therapeutic session. This uniqueness has also been termed "salience" by Weinrach (1994). Salience refers to the idea that clients may identify themselves as part of their culture, or subculture, and may therefore see the world through the perspective that culture, or

---

[3] Please note that by doing good REBT the authors do NOT mean either doing a bad imitation of Albert Ellis or using the "Gloria" tape transcripts as a model of what modern REBT is like. This latter approach was used by one of the two published articles on the effectiveness of REBT with cross-cultural clients. The author (Waxer, 1989) gave 75 Cantonese and 45 Canadian students transcripts of both Ellis' and Rogers' sessions with Gloria and discovered that Canadians were more willing to see Rogers than Ellis, and that Cantonese were less "condemning"of Ellis' style than the Canadians.

subculture, provides. This salience or uniqueness only tends to be apparent when the individual is aware of his minority status within a community (Spires & Robin, 1988). As Spires and Robin (1988) have pointed out there are no Irish in Ireland, but there are Catholics (as well as Protestants).

The authors of the present article (one a Russian, Hungarian, Italian Jew from Brooklyn; the other an Italian Catholic from Pennsylvania) have themselves been known to remark that they never act as "ethnic" at home as they have been known to act when someone points out how different they are. In fact, the senior author has been observed using either "Jackie Masonisms" or the "deez, dem, doze" of the stereotypical Italo-American from Brooklyn in response to either, "How does a Jew feel about . . .?", or, "So, you come from Brooklyn. I thought all Brooklynites . . .".

Dealing with Cultural Uniqueness in REBT

By cultural uniqueness we mean that the client, by virtue of her cultural differences relative to the therapist, may either view herself as a unique individual in the therapist's life, or may view her culture as providing her with unique attributes. This awareness of her own uniqueness may then serve as an Activating Event about which the client may hold both rational and irrational beliefs. We would recommend that the therapist not only should be aware of this possibility, but that the therapist might wish to advance hypotheses about it if the client seems to have trouble establishing a therapeutic alliance.

In our work with clients from ethnically diverse backgrounds we have often had to work on issues related to their actual or perceived cultural uniqueness. One typical way this issue asserts itself begins with the client referring to himself as a member of a particular group or subgroup, e.g., "Look, I am from Puerto Rico and . . ." or, "Baptists believe . . ." In this way they signal us that they think their ethnicity or other area of diversity provides them with some unusual "spin" on the empirical reality that they are presenting. By telling us this they provide us with an entrance into what *they* perceive to be their culture's impact on their present problem. This alerts the culturally "sensitive" therapist to ask for more information about the client's reality within that culture, or other area of diversity. It provides therapists with a golden opportunity to inform themselves about the limits and flexibility of the client's belief system. It also provides an opportunity to assess one potential source of resistance, i.e., "How can I work with you and agree upon a goal for therapy, or continue working towards an agreed-upon goal when you and I are so different? Is it your intention to homogenize me and make me less like me and more like you?"

This last issue is not a trivial one: clients from culturally diverse backgrounds, who see their diversity as both salient and a source of uniqueness, may be reluctant to make therapeutically useful changes if they first make themselves anxious that the therapist's hidden agenda is for them to lose their cultural identity. This accusation is not leveled lightly. The senior author has treated many middle-aged gay and lesbian clients whose previous therapists wanted to "cure" their sexual orientation and ignored the very real problems they wanted to work on in therapy. These previous therapists assumed that their sexual orientation was the problem for these clients—not their depression or their individually problematic ways of dealing with relationships. Hispanic and Afro-American clients have also maintained that their previous therapists saw their culture and cultural values as being the problem. We term this form of therapist response "Therapeutic Imperialism."

Therapeutic Imperialism

Therapeutic Imperialism occurs when a therapist *a priori* views a client's ethnicity, or other area of diversity, as dysfunctional and tries to "cure" her of it; or unilaterally tries to set the therapeutic goal so that the client ultimately thinks, acts, and feels like a "real American."

We are not saying that the goal of assimilating into the mainstream of the culture in which the client lives is either unworthy or dysfunctional, but rather that one has to be clear on whose goal it is. Some culturally diverse clients may have already achieved that goal and may not need, or want, further help. Other culturally diverse clients may wish to assimilate into the mainstream, and indeed may come into therapy for help in making a more rapid or "pain-free" transition. Still other culturally diverse clients are questioning whether or not assimilating is a personally appropriate goal for them. Here too, the therapist can offer both culturally sensitive and therapeutically pragmatic interventions by teaching the client how to use a hedonic calculus for the purposes of value clarification. The therapist has the client examine the potential benefits derived from the status quo, as compared to the potential benefits derived from changes brought about through assimilating into the mainstream. Next, the client is instructed to compare the potential, or actual, drawbacks to the status quo, as compared to the potential, or actual, drawbacks to assimilating. After this is done the client, as well as the therapist, may have a better idea of what is "at stake" in making such a change.

However, whether or not the therapist or the client overtly raises the issue of assimilation within the dominant culture, it may prove to be a covert issue that impacts on the course of treatment, and therefore may become an area that the sensitive therapist needs to offer a hypothesis about. In other words, the sensitive therapist might wish to ask if the client perceives a given intervention as placing him "at risk" with regard to his place within his cultural community. One way in which this "risk" typically manifests itself is in the client's concern about an area we call "congruence" (Robin & DiGiuseppe, 1995).

Congruence

Congruence refers to a process that individuals go through as they become integrated within their own, or some new, culture. Three different cognitive/behavioral issues have been identified: *Cultural congruence, cultural incongruence,* and *Super ethnic* (Robin & DiGiuseppe, 1995).

Cultural congruence refers to the attempt to engage in behaviors, cognitions, and emotions deemed appropriate by the culture. Most people within the culture work towards cultural congruence. When a person's behaviors, cognitions, and emotions are different from but not necessarily disapproved of by those within her own culture, we refer to it as *cultural incongruence. Super ethnic* behavior occurs when the individual's behavior, cognitions, and emotions appear to be rigidly and obsessively culturally congruent. The super ethnic is more American than the Americans, more Irish than the Irish, etc.

Many clients for whom culture is salient are concerned about acting in a culturally congruent way. They attempt to act in accordance with their culture, wherever they are currently living. If they live in their culture of origin, they may rarely run the risk of appearing culturally incongruent. However, if they are too rigid in their beliefs, they do run the risk of being super ethnic and then experiencing incongruity from that vantage point; if they are asked to change even one iota of their rigidly held beliefs they become anxious and angry because they are no longer behaving in a culturally congruent way (as they *think* they must).

Additionally, when they emigrate, or travel abroad, they discover that there are two or more cultures that may require congruent behavior: their culture of origin, and their culture of residence. Thus, many culturally diverse clients have the opportunity to disturb themselves in a number of ways:

1. By demanding that they *must* behave exactly as they did back home, in their culture of origin;
2. By demanding that they *must* behave perfectly like the people in their culture of residence; and
3. By demanding that the people in the culture of residence behave like the people back home.

These demands sometimes operate simultaneously and may lead individuals into anger, anxiety, and depression: *Anger* at themselves and others for not behaving as they should, *anxiety* about the consequences of the potential loss of cultural uniqueness/salience when new ways are adopted, and *depression* about the potential loss of worth or esteem that perceived loss of culture may bring.

Furthermore, the client may experience anxiety about the economic and social consequences of appearing culturally incongruent, both in terms of the culture of origin and the culture of residence.

Other issues that may arise in working with culturally diverse clients are summarized in Table 3.1.

A number of items in the table have already been elaborated upon; there are a few more important elements that bear discussion. In particular, it is advisable for therapists to: (1) admit ignorance, (2) collect data about the client's cultural reality, and (3) refrain from disputing the client's cultural reality and instead *dispute the client's* assumptions *about his/her reality*.

Admit Ignorance

While we have all been trained to be skilled practitioners, we have not been trained to be omniscient. Although we may like to pretend that we are well-educated, our ignorance is daunting. We do not know

Table 3.1   REBT with Culturally Diverse Clients

1. **Develop a Cross-Cultural Therapeutic Alliance**

    a. Gather data about *client's expectations* about therapeutic process.

    b. Educate the client about *therapist's expectations* about therapeutic process.

    c. *Establish alliance.*

        i.   Agree the problem
        ii. Agree the goal
        iii. Establish metaphoric/linguistic rapport

    d. Recognize and deal with common difficulties in establishing cross-cultural alliance.

        i. *Therapist Issues* Most therapists, according to Sue & Sue (1990):

            (1) Expect verbal and emotional expressiveness
            (2) Expect self-disclosure
            (3) Have a Cause/Effect orientation (use the scientific method)
            (4) Make distinction between Mental & Physical Functioning
            (5) Work towards "insight"

        ii. Client Issues

            (1) Shame/guilt about having emotional disturbance
            (2) Shame/guilt about seeking help
            (3) Will psychotherapy "do" anything?—How can talking help?
            (4) Do I agree with therapist's definition of health? In order to be healthy will I have to:

                (a) lose my identity?
                (b) become less ethnic?
                (c) become American or act/think like my therapist?

            (5) Will therapist appreciate and understand my religious and cultural concerns or will s/he belittle them or sneer at them?
            (6) If I come from Third World am I a second-class client with "quaint" ideas?

    e. Stay engaged with the client.

    f. Use active listening.

    g. Do not mix metaphors.

    h. Collect data about client's cultural reality.

    i. ADMIT IGNORANCE.

    j. ALTER STYLE AND PACING TO FIT CLIENTS: Be willing to go slow and Dispute Your Own LFT.

Table 3.1   *(continued)*

2. **Accept client's cultural reality**

   a. Do not dispute reality of the Activating Event.

   b. The client's reality is real for client when the client acts "as if" it is real.

3. **Dispute the A/C connection.**

4. **Dispute the client's *assumptions*** about his/her cultural reality when they connect with dysfunctional outcomes for client.

Note. From *Using Rational-Emotive Therapy With Culturally Diverse Clients,* by M. W. Robin, R. DiGiuseppe, and A. M. Kopec, 1993a, July. Workshop presented at the Third Annual European Congress of Psychology, Tampere, Finland. Adapted with permission.

everything! Let your clients be your guides to their culture. Admit that you do not know.

You should be aware, however, that admitting ignorance can sometimes backfire if the client has rigidly held expectations that you, as the therapist, must be knowledgeable about everything. The approach we advocate is to discuss the limits of your expertise, but reassure the client that while you may not be well informed about her culture, you are well-trained as a practitioner.

Collect Data about the Client's Cultural Reality

We are not suggesting that you expect the client to be a stereotype of her particular culture, or that every client is highly knowledgeable about the formal aspects of her culture. Rather, we are recommending that you ask the client about the salient aspects of her experience within that culture. Ask if this experience is typical of other people within that culture. This question is especially helpful if the client tells you that "We always do it that way back home." You could then ask, "Was there no variation in how it was done?" This gives clients the opportunity to acknowledge that their experience was atypical in some ways.

Many people also have deeply felt religious convictions. Being religious is not, in and of itself, dysfunctional and is not always associated with emotional disturbance (Robin & DiGiuseppe, unpublished manuscript submitted for publication in 1995). Ask about the importance of transcendent experiences to your client. Familiarize yourself with the basic tenets of her religious/cultural belief system, including healing practices and expectations about how the healing process is conducted (Boyer, 1983; Beutler, Mohr, Grawe, & Engle, 1991; Jilek, 1986). Where it is appropriate, we believe that culturally sensitive therapists should encourage their clients to explore the usefulness of traditional healing methods as an adjunct to therapy. This doesn't mean that the therapist should encourage the client to engage in practices that may be self-harming or proven to be ineffective, but rather that the therapist should explore the efficacy of particular healing traditions. We have found that by opening the door to this sort of dialogue we enhance the therapeutic alliance, acknowledge the client's value system, and admit that there are many ways of effective healing. Even if you personally believe that some traditional methods are nothing more than placebos, keep in mind that even placebos have been shown to be effective in controlled studies.

Do Not Dispute the Client's Cultural Reality, but Do Dispute the Client's *Assumptions* about His/Her Cultural Reality

Once again we are pointing out that doing good cross-cultural therapy is doing good REBT—don't dispute the activating event, dispute the irrational belief. In practice, this recommendation encourages the culturally sensitive REBT practitioner to operate from the assumption that the client is accurately describing her cultural reality *as she perceives it*. Rather than disputing that reality, or rather the accuracy of the client's perception of reality, we feel that the better choice is to dispute the client's distorted inferences, attributions, and irrational beliefs which are based on that reality.

The senior author once had the occasion to work with Y. A., a man from the Middle East, who was very anxious and depressed. Y. A. had just proposed to a woman for the second time and was panicked that if she didn't accept him he would never have a wife. Rather than immediately dispute what appeared to be his obviously irrational belief that if one woman did not accept his proposal then he could never get another woman, I inquired about his background. Y. A. told me that in the community that he came from, it was customary for males of his class and status to have a bride selected for them. If he was attracted to the prospective bride, he was expected to offer a proposal which she was required to refuse. This gave them both a moment to reconsider their options. If upon further reflection he was still interested he could propose a second time. If she was interested, she could accept and he was committed to marry her. She could refuse this second offer if she wanted more information about him or if she had a "better" offer. He could accept her refusal without loss of status or opportunity, but if he persisted in a third proposal—which he was more or less obliged to offer, as a man of honor—and was refused again, the matchmakers would not offer him a second chance.

I had a number of ways I could respond to this, but decided to first gather more information about Y. A.'s culture. I asked him to tell me the social consequences for men who had been accepted as well as for men who had been refused. I asked about exceptions to the rule. I asked about emotional "scripts" (i.e., are panic, depression, and anxiety required by the culture for men in his situation?).

By gathering this additional information, I was able to discover that there were exceptions to the rule; that he could marry a woman of lower status, that those marriages were sometimes stronger than the ones of equal status, and that men of honor did not always propose a third time. I then took him through a hedonic calculus which examined a number of available options: propose a third time; do not propose a third time; and—since he was expecting to settle in the US and not return home—look for a woman here who might not share his beliefs, but who might share his life. For each of the elements in the decision matrix, we examined the possible costs and benefits. We also examined the emotional outcomes for each element.

The client was helped to see that he could behave in a culturally congruent way and still not propose. He was also helped to see that while the outcome of refusal was unpleasant, it was not as bad as he had assumed. He decided, that since he did like the girl, he would propose a third time and dispute the awfulness of a possible refusal. He also decided that if he was refused he would look for a woman of status in this country who would not be required to see him as a "loser." And lastly, he decided that even if he was refused, he was not required by either his culture of origin or his culture of residence to see himself as a reject but only as a frustrated suitor—and that was a description he could live with if things did not work out. These decisions helped him overcome his anxiety, panic, and depression.

In the following section, a detailed case presentation is provided. This case highlights some of the issues that are typical of our work with culturally diverse clients.

"Shoya moya ik baraba": THE CASE OF A. Z.

A. Z., age 32, was a man from the Indian subcontinent who had been living in the U.S. for the last 10 years. He reluctantly sought therapy from the senior author because the employee assistance program in his office recommended that he either get help or change jobs. He was highly irascible on the job, had difficulty concentrating, and appeared to be "lost in a fog."

The Initial Session

When he came in for our first visit, A. Z. seemed to be somewhat upset that I appeared to be Jewish. I agreed with him and made the comment that not only did I appear to be Jewish but that, in fact, I was Jewish. He said he didn't know if this was a good idea because he was a believer in Allah and our peoples were at war. I told him that I identified myself as an American and that his country and America were not at war. I also asked him if we needed to be mistrustful of each other just because some of the believers in Allah and Israel were at war. He took that in and said that he wasn't sure that the ideas of a Jew would be compatible with his own. The following dialogue ensued:

DR. R: Do you read the Koran?

A. Z.:   Yes, it is a source of inspiration to me!

DR. R: Doesn't the Koran accept the teachings of Moses, and treat him as a prophet?

A. Z.:   Yes, it does.

DR. R: Would it therefore be inappropriate for you to work with and possibly benefit from someone who also accepts the teachings of Moses? While I am no prophet, mightn't my being Jewish be beneficial?

A. Z.:   It might, but what happens if I disagree with you?

DR. R: When you ask me that question, what are you trying to tell me?

A. Z.:   Aren't I supposed to follow your advice? Won't you be angry with me if I disagree with you, or ignore your advice?

DR. R: Advice is just that—*advice*. It is a *suggestion* about how to behave differently. My suggestions do not have the force of Mosaic law. They are not commandments. If you ignore them I will not respond like either G–d or Moses. Therefore, if you disagree, or choose to do something different, what is the worst that could happen?

The session continued with me outlining what he could expect from me as an REBT therapist, and what I would expect from him as an REBT client. I also outlined the process of identifying and disputing only those beliefs that would get him into either emotional or behavioral trouble in his daily life. He seemed interested in this process, and said he liked the idea of being vigilant about wrong thinking. He did, however, express some additional concerns:

> A. Z.:   We have a saying in my country, "Shoya moya ik baraba": A sleeping man and a dead man are the same. If you are dead or asleep you can't be vigilant. I like the idea of being vigilant about my thoughts. But what will happen if I learn from you? I am a Moslem from India and you are a Westerner and a Jew. Are you going to try to turn me into you?

A. Z.'s last question was a good one. It was also a question that we have been asked, in one form or another, by clients who come from many different cultures, religions, and ethnicities. We have been asked this question by feminists who challenged us on our sensitivity to women. We have been asked this question by gay and lesbian clients, who were concerned that heterosexual therapists would challenge not only their screwy thinking, but also the validity of their sexual orientation.

If A. Z. had been from our dominant culture, I would have been tempted to view his interrogation of me, and the reports of his irascibility on the job, as symptomatic of either a borderline personality disorder or paranoia. I would have been wrong on both counts. I tentatively hypothesized that his questions were congruent with someone who might be feeling "at risk" both personally and culturally, and was therefore rightly asking to be reassured that I was not antagonistic to him or his culture. At the end of our first session, I tentatively diagnosed him as suffering from anxiety and/or depression.

During my first session with A. Z., I had the opportunity to gather information about some of his expectations about therapy. I also took advantage of the opportunity to educate A. Z. about the process of REBT. I had worked with other Islamic clients, and they had taught me about their religion, and I had had occasion to read the Koran. Based on my previous experiences, I formulated a number of questions that I planned to pursue in subsequent sessions:

1. How salient is A. Z.'s culture of origin? Does A. Z. intend to try to assimilate?

2. Is A. Z. religiously observant? If so, then how does he deal with the hundreds of commandments that are expected of the observant? Does he treat these commandments as suggestions or *musts*?

3. Does A. Z. assume, as other recent immigrants occasionally do, that people in the U.S. are as rigorously rule-bound as he is? How does he evaluate our relative freedom?

4. What effect, if any, does our relative freedom have on the way he evaluates himself and others?

Later Sessions

Across several subsequent sessions, I was able to learn the answers to the questions listed above. As I had suspected, A. Z.'s culture of origin was highly salient for him, and he was rather concerned that he would lose his cultural identity through ongoing exposure to his culture of residence. He was indeed religiously observant, and viewed the commandments contained within the Koran as a series of absolutistic musts. This view, however, was not limited to the area of religious observance; A. Z. also tended to view the behavioral prescriptions of his home community and culture as being absolutistic rules that *had to* be followed. In addition, A. Z. believed that the Americans with whom he came in contact would be just as rule-bound as he was. He did, in fact, erroneously assume that these other individuals would follow many of the same rules as he did. As will be seen, a number of these issues became the focus of treatment as my work with A. Z. proceeded.

Uniqueness issues. A. Z. and I frequently had to work on his uniqueness issues. He not only was aware of his difference from me, but assumed that this difference was remarked upon by others whom he would casually pass by on the street. A. Z.'s uniqueness or salience issues could have been misdiagnosed as paranoia if I had not been aware that despite his having lived in the U.S. for many years, he strongly identified with his culture of origin as well as his community of origin. A. Z. came from a small town where he and his family were well known. He knew from direct experience that he and his family's behavior, dress, and appearance were subjects of community interest and discussion. Furthermore, he knew that his community taught its members to be vigilant about strangers.

Since A. Z.'s culture was very salient to him, his uniqueness was also salient; he believed that everyone would be aware of him, either because he was "important" or because he was a stranger. I was able to get him to gather data that helped him see that not only were the streets of New York City filled with people from many different cultures, and most "native New Yorkers" were born somewhere else, but that being different—at least in New York City—was the norm and therefore unremarked upon. We then went on to examine his *shoulds* about whether or not he should be the center of attention. He remarked that it was odd that he felt that way, because one of the reasons he had left home was to distance himself from all the prying eyes of his small town. He assumed that his importance at home as well as his strangeness here was as apparent to passersby as it was to him. I helped him see that he was making himself disturbed by assuming that people in New York City *should* act like people at home.

A. Z. was also helped to see that one of the causes of his problems at work was his belief that everyone was as concerned about his strangeness as he would himself have been about strangers at home. He was helped to see that vigilance about strangers, while possibly useful in his village at home, might not be so useful in the context of his workplace in New York City. This discovery about how vigilance might be dysfunctional in New York led to another period of distrust and a potential weakening of the therapeutic alliance.

A. Z. the Super Ethnic. A. Z. now began to worry that I was trying to get him to stop being "himself." Although he now acknowledged the view that a high level of vigilance could be quite unhelpful within his culture of residence, the very fact that I had shown him this alternative perspective led him to become newly suspicious of my motives as his therapist.

A. Z. appeared to subscribe to the following irrational belief: "I *must* maintain a high state of vigilance toward 'strangers' at all times; the consequences of failing to do so would be *awful!*" Importantly, he also thought that other people in his work environment held the very same belief. Thus, he was constantly preoccupied with scrutinizing *them* because he was certain that they were scrutinizing *him!* In the exchange that follows, I attempt to help A. Z. see how he could modify his beliefs without giving up a personally valued aspect of his cultural identity.

> A. Z.:   If I give up this belief, I'm abandoning the teachings of my community.
>
> DR. R: How does that follow?
>
> A. Z.:   We are taught to be cautious with strangers. If I give up my caution, won't I have to behave like you and not like me?
>
> DR. R: I am not asking you to act like me, I am only pointing out that people in your office may not have been taught to be as cautious and mistrustful as you were. I am asking you to accept their behavior and not assume that they are as mistrustful of you as you have been taught to be of them.
>
> A. Z.:   You mean I can accept that they are not as suspicious of me as I would be of them?
>
> DR. R: Yes, that's right.
>
> A. Z.:   OK, I see that if I did that I would be less distracted and anxious at work, because I wouldn't be saying to myself "I had better watch my step because they are always watching me." But, if I give up this belief, won't I have to stop thinking like I was raised?
>
> DR. R: I don't see how that follows. You can still think like you were raised while granting others the right to think like they were raised.
>
> A. Z.:   Good, because I don't want to give up my background.

A. Z.'s belief that he would have to lose his identity, or give up his background, when he changed one of his core beliefs was not unique to him, as we discussed earlier. A. Z., when asked about the community norm of vigilance, described his family as more vigilant than most, and noted that this was remarked about in the village. I was able to get him to see that by moderating his own vigilance he was not giving up his ethnic identity, but was becoming more like the rest of his cultural community.

Once A. Z. was able to moderate his vigilance, and was no longer Super Ethnic but rather culturally congruent, he came out of his fog. He discovered that he had more time to pay attention to work-related issues. He also became more sociable on the job. This transformation occurred as he learned to accept his co-workers as individuals. He no longer condemned them for not being like the people in his village.

CONCLUSION

As you can see from the foregoing case examples, REBT can be appropriately used with culturally diverse clients. The additions or modifications that need to be made to our already existing procedures are:

1. To ask the client what she expects therapy to be like;
2. To alert the client as to what is expected in a typical session;
3. To be willing to admit ignorance;
4. To develop a more laid-back style while gathering data so that you can understand more about the client's uniqueness/salience and congruence issues; and
5. To dispute only those inferences and beliefs about the client's cultural reality that are associated with dysfunctional consequences.

As therapists, it is quite likely that at various points we will be working with individuals whose cultural background differs from our own. Given this likelihood, it is advisable for each of us to become more culturally sensitive. With this goal in mind, we have included a list of helpful books and articles that follows the *References* section of this chapter.

We would, however, caution the reader against believing that cultural sensitivity is a state that can be attained though mere exposure to a set of published resources. Rather, cultural sensitivity is a *process* that is continually refined through the assimilation of new experiences. Although one can develop *expertise* in working with culturally diverse clients, it is probably best to refrain from regarding oneself as an "expert."

One final note: When you encounter difficulties in working with clients from diverse cultural backgrounds, seek supervision from a fellow rational-emotive practitioner. Knowledgeable peers represent one of the most important clinical resources we have at our disposal (Robin, Weinrach, & Morris, 1994).

REFERENCES

Atkinson, D. R., Morten, G., & Sue, D. W. (1989). *Counseling American minorities: A cross-cultural perspective* (3rd ed.). Dubuque, IA: Brown.

Beck, A. T. (1976). *Cognitive therapy and the emotional disorders*. Madison, CT: International Universities Press.

Beck, A. T. (1983). Cognitive therapy of depression: New perspectives. In P. Clayton (Ed.), *Treatment of depression: Old controversies and new approaches* (pp. 265–290). New York: Raven.

Beutler, L. E., Mohr, D. C., Grawe, K., & Engle, D. (1991). Looking for differential treatment effects: Cross-cultural predictors of differential psychotherapy efficacy. *Journal of Psychotherapy Integration, 1*(2), 121–141.

Boyer, L. (1983). Approaching cross-cultural psychotherapy. *Journal of Psychoanalytic Anthropology, 6*(3), 237–245.

Cherbosque, J. (1987). Differential effects of counselor self-disclosure statements on perception of the counselor and willingness to disclose: A cross-cultural study. *Psychotherapy, 24*(3), 434–437.

Chessler, P. (1972). *Women and madness.* Garden City, NY: Doubleday.

Christensen, E. W. (1989). Counseling Puerto Ricans: Some cultural considerations. *Personnel and Guidance Journal, 55,* 412–415.

Deane, F. P. (1992). Pretreatment expectations of New Zealand clients receiving cognitive/behavioural psychotherapy: Comparison with a North American sample. *International Journal of Social Psychiatry, 38*(2), 138–149.

DiGiuseppe, R., Robin, M. W., & Dryden, W. (1990). Rational-emotive therapy and the Judeo-Christian tradition: A focus on clinical strategies. *Journal of Cognitive Psychotherapy: An International Quarterly, 4,* 355–368.

Ellis, A. (1977). *Reason and emotion in psychotherapy.* Secaucus, NJ: Citadel.

Ellis, A. (1989). Rational-emotive therapy. In R. J. Corsini & D. Wedding (Eds.), *Current psychotherapies* (4th ed.), (pp. 197–238). Itasca, IL: Peacock.

Ellis, A. (1991). The revised ABC's of rational-emotive therapy (RET). *Journal of Rational-Emotive and Cognitive Behavior Therapy, 9,* 139–172.

Freud, S. (1938). Totem and taboo. In A. A. Brill (Ed.), *The basic writings of Sigmund Freud* (pp. 807–930). New York: Modern Library. (Original work published 1912)

Freud, S. (1962). *Civilization and its discontents.* New York: W. W. Norton. (Original work published 1930)

Hollingshead, A. B., & Redlich, F. C. (1958). *Social class and mental illness: A community study.* New York: Wiley.

Jilek, W. G. (1986). Witchcraft and psychotherapy. *British Journal of Psychiatry, 149,* 796–797.

Landrine, H. (1992). Clinical implications of cultural differences: The referential versus the indexical self. *Clinical Psychology Review, 12,* 401–415.

Lefley, H. P. (1989). Empirical support for credibility and giving in cross-cultural psychotherapy. *American Psychologist, 44,* 1163.

Malinowski, B. (1927). *Sex and repression in savage society.* New York: Harcourt.

Pedersen, P. (Ed.) (1985). *Handbook of cross-cultural counseling and therapy.* Westport, CT: Greenwood Press.

Robin, M. W. (1992, July). *Rational-emotive therapy with culturally diverse clients.*

Clinical seminar presented at the Institute for Rational-Emotive Therapy, New York, NY.

Robin, M. W., & DiGiuseppe, R. (1995). Endorsing irrational beliefs crossculturally: Clinical implications. In L. Loeb-Adler & B. Runi Mukhurji (Eds.), *The spirit vs the scalpel: Traditional healing and modern psychotherapy* (pp. 147–165). New York: Greenwood Press/Praeger.

Robin, M. W., DiGiuseppe, R., & Alvarez, F. (1991a, July). *Endorsement of irrational/rational beliefs: Cross-cultural & cross-ethnic implications for mental & emotional health.* Paper presented at the 23rd Interamerican Congress of Psychology, San Jose, Costa Rica.

Robin, M. W., DiGiuseppe, R., & Alvarez, F. (1991b, July). *Using rationalemotive therapy with culturally diverse clients.* Workshop presented at the 23rd Interamerican Congress of Psychology, San Jose, Costa Rica.

Robin, M. W., DiGiuseppe, R., & Kopec, A. M. (1993a, July). *Using rationalemotive therapy with culturally diverse clients.* Workshop presented at the Third Annual European Congress of Psychology, Tampere, Finland.

Robin, M. W., DiGiuseppe, R., & Kopec, A. M. (1993b, July). *Measuring irrational beliefs: Cross-cultural implications.* Poster session presented at the Third Annual European Congress of Psychology, Tampere, Finland.

Robin, M. W., Weinrach, S., & Morris, G. B. (1994, October). *Cultural diversity.* Workshop presented at the Refresher Practicum, Institute for Rational-Emotive Therapy, New York, NY.

Robin, M. W., & DiGiuseppe, R. Manuscript submitted for publication in 1995. *Irrationality, religiosity, and religious observance.*

Simola, S. (1992). Differences among sexist, nonsexist, and feminist family therapies. *Professional Psychology: Research and Practice, 23*(5), 376–381.

Spires, R. C., & Robin, M. W. (1988, April). *The construction of ethnic identity.* Paper presented at the Conference on Cross-Cultural Research sponsored by the Institute for Cross-Cultural and Cross-Ethnic Studies of Molloy College at Pennsylvania State University, State College, PA.

Sue, D. W., Bernier, J. E., Durran, A., Feinberg, L., Pedersen, P., Smith, E. J., & Vasquez-Nuttall, E. (1981). A position paper: Cross-cultural counseling competencies: Education and training committee, Division 17, A.P.A. *The Counseling Psychologist, 10*(2), 45–52.

Sue, D. W., & Sue, D. (1990). *Counseling the culturally different: Theory & practice* (2nd ed.). New York: Wiley.

Sue, S., & Zane, N. (1987). The role of culture and cultural techniques in psychotherapy: A critique and reformulation. *American Psychologist, 42*(1), 37–45

Waxer, P. H. (1989). Cantonese versus Canadian evaluation of directive and non-directive therapy. *Canadian Journal of Counseling, 23*(3), 263–272.

Weinrach, S. (1994, October). *Comments on cultural diversity.* Workshop,

Cultural Diversity, Refresher Practicum, Institute for Rational-Emotive Therapy, New York, NY.

SOME USEFUL BOOKS/ARTICLES

Atkinson, D. R., Casas, A., & Abreu, J. (1992). Mexican-American acculturation, counselor ethnicity and cultural sensitivity, and perceived counselor competence. *Journal of Counseling Psychology, 39*(4), 515–520.

Atkinson, D. R., Morten, G., & Sue, D. W. (1989). A minority identity development model. In D. R. Atkinson, G. Morten, & D. W. Sue (Eds.), *Counseling American minorities* (pp. 35–52). Dubuque, IA: W. C. Brown.

Axelson, J. A. (1993). *Counseling and development in a multicultural society* (2nd ed.). Pacific Grove, CA: Brooks Cole.

Brislin, R. W. (1981). *Cross-cultural encounters: Face to face interaction.* New York: Pergamon.

Budman, C. L., Lipson, J. G., & Meleis, A. I. (1992). The cultural consultant in mental health care: The case of an Arab adolescent. *American Journal of Orthopsychiatry, 62*(3), 359–370.

Canino, I. A., Rubio-Stipec, M., Canino, G., & Escobar, J. (1992). Functional somatic symptoms: A cross-ethnic comparison. *American Journal of Orthopsychiatry, 62*(4), 605–612.

Foulks, E. F., Merkel, L, & Boehnlein, J. K. (1992). Symptoms in nonpatient Southeast Asian refugees. *The Journal of Nervous and Mental Disease, 180*(7), 466–468.

Gibbs, J. T., & Huang, L. N. (Eds.). (1989). *Children of color: Psychological interventions with minority youth.* San Francisco: Jossey-Bass.

Harkness, S. (1992). Cross-cultural research in child development: A sample of the state of the art. *Developmental Psychology, 28*(4), 622–625.

Henderson, G., & Primeaux, M. (1981). *Transcultural health care.* Menlo Park, CA: Addison-Wesley.

Heras, P. (1992). Cultural considerations in the assessment and treatment of child sexual abuse. *Journal of Child Sexual Abuse, 1*(3), 119–132.

Jenkins, A. H. (1988). *The psychology of the Afro-American: A humanistic experience.* New York: Pergamon. (Original work published 1982)

Kleinman, A., & Good, B. (Eds.). (1985). *Culture and depression: Studies in the anthropology and cross-cultural psychiatry of affect and disorder.* Berkeley, CA: University of California Press.

Lin, K. M., Lau, J. K. C., Yamamoto, J., Zheng, Y. P., Kim, H. S., Cho, H., & Nakasaki, G. (1992). Hwa-Byung: A community study of Korean Americans. *The Journal of Nervous and Mental Disease, 180*(6), 386–391.

Martin, J. K., & Nagayama Hall, G. C. N. (1992). Thinking black, thinking internal, thinking feminist. *Journal of Counseling Psychology, 39*(4), 509–514.

Mesquita, B., & Frijda., N. (1992). Cultural variations in emotions: A review. *Psychological Bulletin, 112*(2), 179–204.

Noh, S., Speechley, M., Kaspar, V., & Zheng, W. (1992). Depression in Korean immigrants in Canada: I. Method of the study and prevalence of depression. *The Journal of Nervous and Mental Disease, 180*(9), 573–577.

Noh, S., Zheng, W., Speechley, M., & Kaspar, V. (1992). Depression in Korean immigrants in Canada: II. Correlates of gender, work and marriage. *The Journal of Nervous and Mental Disease, 180*(9), 578–582.

Payer, L. (1988). *Medicine & culture: Varieties of treatment in the United States, England, West Germany, and France.* New York: Henry Holt.

Price, B. K., & McNeill, E. (1992). Cultural commitment and attitudes toward seeking counseling services in American Indian college students. *Professional Psychology: Research and Practice, 23*(5), 376–381.

Roberts, R. E. (1992). Manifestation of depressive symptoms among adolescents: A comparison of Mexican Americans with the majority and other minority populations. *The Journal of Nervous and Mental Disease, 180*(10), 627–633.

Russel, J. A. (1991). Culture and the categorization of emotions. *Psychological Bulletin, 110*(3), 426–450.

Segall, M. H., Dasen, P. R., Berry, J. W., & Poortinga, Y. H. (1990). *Human behavior in global perspective: An introduction to cross-cultural psychology.* New York: Pergamon.

Tharp, R. G. (1990). Cultural diversity and treatment of children. *Journal of Consulting and Clinical Psychology, 59*(6), 799–812.

Tseng, W. S., Masahiro, A., Kitanishi, K., McLaughlin, D. G., & Kyomen, H. (1992). Diagnostic patterns of social-phobia: Comparisons in Tokyo & Hawaii. *The Journal of Nervous and Mental Disease, 180*(7), 466–468.

CHAPTER 4

Using REBT with Clients with Disabilities

Rochelle Balter

According to the United States Department of Commerce (1995) and Dorge (1995), more than 10% of the United States population has an overt disability at any point in time. An even larger percentage of the population (Dorge, 1995) has "invisible disabilities," such as diabetes, heart disease, epilepsy, emphysema, HIV/AIDS, and learning disabilities. The number of elderly people with disabilities is even greater, with some disabilities, such as hearing loss, found in over 50% of the population over 70 years of age (Dorge, 1995). Similar statistics regarding disability probably exist worldwide. Therefore, psychologists will be seeing more and more patients with disabilities.

This chapter will define disabilities; look at various factors affecting disabilities and people with disabilities; and will examine attitudes toward those having a disability. It will then explore the use of rational emotive behavior therapy with clients with disabilities and will present a case illustrating the use of this approach with a client with a physical disability.

DEFINING DISABILITIES

Disability is truly unique in that no one is immune. Anyone of any income level, education level, intelligence, race, religion, or gender identification is equally likely to experience a disability at some time. According to the statistics cited (Dorge, 1995), almost everyone alive will experience a disability at some time during his or her lifetime. Since Western society places so much emphasis on an intact and attractive physique, and often devalues those that do not meet this standard, those with disabilities frequently encounter disdain, fear, and avoidance.

How do we define disability? According to many sources, including the Americans with Disabilities Act (ADA) (1990), a disability is any physical, emotional, or cognitive limitation in functioning that interferes with one or more activities of daily living. Activities of daily living include the ability to get up in the morning and prepare for the day, feed oneself, get to work, pay one's bills, raise a family, engage in social activities, etc.

As was previously mentioned, disabilities may be overt and readily apparent, or they may not be immediately apparent to others. Each classification of disability has its own set of complicating factors. The early literature on disabilities (Shontz, 1975; Siller, 1976; Wright, 1960; Yuker et al., 1960) tended to look at the treatment of those with disabilities as a uniform phenomenon with shared problems, stages, and solutions. The uniqueness of each person's condition, problems, and situation was not taken into account.

Sweetland (1990) differentiated between chronic illness and disability. He pointed out that the two may overlap in some cases and that many with chronic illnesses, such as diabetes or multiple sclerosis, will have disabling conditions concomitant to their illnesses. However, those with a primarily physical disability usually have an area which is disabled, such as one or more affected limbs, or an area of the body that is paralyzed or paretic, but in general, their health is often excellent. The effect of the disability is not always changeable or degenerative. It can often be stable. Other differences exist in the ways in which those with chronic illnesses and permanent disabilities need to adapt their lives to accommodate their disabilities. Ellis (Rubin, Walen, & Ellis, 1990) stated that there is no vacation from diabetes. This is also true of permanent disabilities such as paraplegia, quadriplegia, and many other conditions.

FACTORS AFFECTING WORKING
WITH CLIENTS WITH DISABILITIES

In working with clients with disabilities, it is important that therapists take a number of factors into account which affect the types of issues that may arise in therapy. Such factors include the following:

Type of Disability

There are many different types of disability. The most commonly mentioned physical disabilities are blindness and visual impairment; deafness and being hard of hearing; and spinal cord injuries and orthopedic disabilities such as paraplegia, quadriplegia, and paresis (weakness of any part of the body). There are different causes for each type of disability and different degrees of functional limitations within each type of physical disability. People with physical disabilities are more heterogeneous than they are homogeneous.

There are also what are known as "invisible disabilities." An invisible disability is one which also limits one's ability to perform activities of daily living, but its restrictions are not as obvious as those disabilities mentioned above. A person who has cardiac problems, diabetes, or emphysema may very well have more functional limitations than an individual who must use a wheelchair because of paralysis; however, unless the person with cardiac problems self-identifies or the person with emphysema or asthma overtly carries an oxygen tank, no one may guess that he or she has a physical disability.

Other conditions considered disabilities under law (ADA) have no overt signs and may be cognitive or emotional in nature. Since they do interfere with activities of daily living, they have been classified as disabilities. These would include the cognitive effects of Alzheimer's disease and other dementias, learning disabilities, and schizophrenia and other mental illnesses.

Age of Onset

A disability with adult onset is very different from a disability that occurred at birth or during childhood. When a disability occurs early in life, adaptation to it is different, and the adaptation is often reflective of the parents' attitudes toward the child with the disability. Sweetland

(1990) points out that most parents hold fantasies about their child's future. When the child is born with a disability or develops a disability in infancy, these fantasies are often smashed. Parents may react with guilt or anger as they mourn the loss of the fantasy. Parents also may encounter pity or awe from other parents about how they deal with their child. The parents' views, if abnormal, may lead to dysfunctional beliefs in the child and paradigms where unrealistic expectations are held of that child. As Sweetland (1990) states, either position may be a disservice to the child who is taught to see the world and its requirements in a distorted fashion.

Ammermann (cited in Martin, 1995) reported on child abuse of children with disabilities and speculated as to whether the disability prompted the abuse. The predictors of abuse he listed in his presentation were:

1.   Disruption of attachment formation—because a child with a disability might be more difficult to hold;

2.   Care burdens—because a child with disabilities might have special needs;

3.   Behavior problems—because children with some specific disabilities, such as attention deficit/hyperactivity disorder, might engage in potentially dangerous or destructive behaviors which raise parental stress levels; and

4.   Communication limitations—which are more frequently seen in speech disabilities and hearing disabilities and may result in a lack of understanding or ability to adequately express needs.

All of the aforementioned, according to Ammermann, may lead to increased problems in parenting and to child abuse for these children.

Adult onset comes with its own set of problems in that one's life is often changed dramatically by the disability. If the individual who acquires the disability is independent and single, a role reversal may occur—often encouraged by the rehabilitation facility—wherein the individual once again becomes dependent on parents that he or she already separated from. If the individual is part of a couple or family, role reversals may occur in which the person who may have been head of household loses that title and becomes dependent on his or her spouse and/or children.

Type of Onset

Traumatic onset, such as spinal cord injury after an accident, is different than loss of function due to a degenerative condition such as multiple sclerosis. Even though the resulting functional limitations may be similar, the time the individual needs to adapt to the disability and the method of adaptation may be quite different.

Education and Occupation

Differences in education and occupation will determine whether a person who has a disability can return to the same type of work that she did before the onset of the disability. If the work was very physical, the person may find that her whole life needs to be changed. The individual may now need to return to school, and may need to change the way in which she views both self and world. This may cause both role stress and family stress.

The Rehabilitation Process

When the disability is traumatic or occurs early in life, the individual with the disability often must go through a rehabilitation program to help in adaptation to the physical/medical aspects of the disability. When the disability has a slow, degenerative onset, rehabilitation is often not an option. This would be true in slowly degenerative conditions, such as amyotrophic lateral sclerosis and the other sclerosing conditions, and in disabilities related to AIDS, wherein the medical system does not see the patient as a rehabilitation candidate because of the projected shortened lifespan. Often the person with traumatic onset, whether old or young, must go through a psychological adaptation process that may take longer than the time allotted for physical rehabilitation, sometimes limiting that person's ability to adequately benefit from the full rehabilitation program.

Calabro (1990) points out that it is during the rehabilitation process that the person with a newly acquired disability learns to adapt not as much to the disability but to the environment which has now radically changed for that individual. Calabro sees the REBT approach as being most helpful in the rehabilitation process. Although Calabro acknowledges the shortcomings of stage theories, he has constructed a very loose general stage theory for the convenience of classifying his approach when working with clients with spinal cord injuries and other physical disabilities. His stage theory for the rehabilitation process begins with a "Pre-encounter Phase" in which the person is first confronted with the new disability and is unable to sustain work on the immediate and realistic Activating Event, but instead panics and catastrophizes regarding anticipated negative Activating Events which spreads back to what is happening in the present. The patient is protected from prolonged exposure to the real situation by both shock and denial. Denial itself, as Calabro (1990) points out, is very complex. It is not only tenacious, but can be of a cooperative or uncooperative nature. When it is cooperative, the patient participates in all the prescribed activities in the rehabilitation program even though the patient states that he will recover and not need the treatment. In uncooperative denial, the patient refuses to participate, and loses out on needed services. The patient may need the support of a mental health professional at this point, but because of the anxiety present that is contained by the denial, the patient often avoids the treating mental health professional.

Calabro's second phase is the "Post-Encounter Phase," which may be characterized by both bargaining behaviors and beliefs and anxiety and depression. Calabro states that during this phase the denial has dissipated enough for the patient to face the disability. The patient is able to fully participate in rehabilitation activities and realistically face the facts of the disability, but still has cognitive distortions concerning future events related to the disability. Calabro warns, however, that it is unwise to confront the patient or strongly dispute irrational beliefs at this time, because doing so might lead to the patient's becoming depressed, angry, or anxious and not engaging in the cooperative behaviors needed to work on physical rehabilitation.

When anxiety and depression do occur, Calabro cautions the therapist about strongly disputing irrational beliefs. Instead, he recommends that the techniques of distraction and reframing be used to keep the patient's focus on the present and away from unrealistic distortions.

The last phase, the "Rational-Reencounter Phase" (Calabro, 1990), is the stage in which most of the active rational emotive behavioral interventions are made. It is characterized by three emotional patterns: (1) primary anxiety—secondary depression; (2) primary depression; and (3) primary depression—secondary anger.

The first pattern, primary anxiety—secondary depression, is concerned with the patient's perceived ability to survive with the disability. The second, primary depression, may be precipitated by a comparison of life prior to the disability with imagined differences in the future as well as an altered sense of self-worth. The primary depression—secondary anger phase is connected to beliefs regarding the fairness principle and how the disability affects interaction with the environment. According to Calabro, however, this stage is hallmarked by a significant change in the patient's perceptions, i.e., insight into the connection between dysfunctional thoughts and dysfunctional feelings, as well as the ability to change these through psychotherapy. The distressing part of this is that this phase is often beginning as the physical rehabilitation phase is ending. Unless the patient is willing to attend psychotherapy as part of an outpatient program, the opportunity is lost to help the patient to change her belief system.

In the early days of physical rehabilitation, the patient was seen as helpless and dependent upon the rehabilitation team for solutions. Patients were not given an active role in their rehabilitation. This is still true in some facilities. In others, however, the patient is given an active role but is discharged before helpful cognitive shifts can be completed.

Support System and Living Arrangements

A person who lives alone and is single often has problems that are very different from those of someone who has the company of others. There is no way of placing a positive or negative valence on either situation, as each person will have different problems that need to be solved. The rationality or irrationality of the members of the support system will also be an important factor; this may determine whether individuals with a disability are treated with respect and dignity, or whether they become the object of the irrational beliefs of those making up the support system.

Emotional and Cognitive Resources

The person's adaptability and premorbid personality will greatly determine the method used to deal with disability. Adaptation to disability, as well as living with a disability, as Ellis (1995) has pointed out, require high frustration tolerance and the will to stop whining and start dealing with hassles and obstacles. If the individual experienced low frustration tolerance, or no frustration tolerance, before having the disability, a great deal of effort may need to be expended to change the individual's way of both viewing and dealing with the world. Both Ellis (1995) and Sweetland (1990) have pointed out that although the individual with a physical disability may no longer be able to achieve mastery over the physical aspects of his world, he can learn to exercise cognitive control, which is usually left intact, unless the injury resulting from the onset of the disability affects the brain. Examples of this are traumatic brain injury (TBI) or the sequelae of meningitis.

Cultural and Religious Beliefs

Different cultures and different religions view disability in different ways. The culture from which the individual comes and the beliefs common to this culture regarding disability will often influence adaptability. For example, many Asian and Spanish cultures tend to view disability in a very negative manner. In order not to alienate the usually strong family support system, patients may not confront others regarding their disability-related beliefs.

    The religious beliefs that the person with a disability holds, as well as the religiosity of the individual, will also impact adaptation. Some religions espouse healing services and the laying on of hands. If a patient with a disability practices such a religion, it is often best not to discourage patient participation in such activities. If the healing does not work, as it often does not, the patient may find it necessary to come to terms with the disability and its implications for her life. Attending healing-oriented meetings may also help to convince family members that the person does want to do something about the disability and is not happy concerning this condition.

    Other religions believe in certain conditions as a punishment for past sins. Such a belief may interfere with patient compliance. The individual may espouse the belief that since the disability must be deserved, necessary physical therapy or physical maintenance programs (e.g., maintaining bowel routines; stretching exercises to prevent contractures; learning to use ASL or Braille) will certainly fail to alleviate the situation. The patient may believe that since the disability has its basis in retribution for sins, help or relief is not deserved and cannot be attained. These beliefs need to be strongly disputed.

The Stage During Which the Individual Comes to Psychotherapy

An individual who is still undergoing rehabilitation will have very different views of life and disability than one who has adapted to or lived with the disability for a period of time. Such individuals will also be very different from those who have lived with a disability since birth or early childhood. Each may have irrational beliefs regarding her disability; however, these beliefs may be distinct and dependent on time of onset of the disability.

Attitudes toward Disability

Another important factor in dealing with disability is that of attitude. As was previously mentioned, society generally views physical perfection as an ideal, and physical disability as negative (Dembo, Levitan, & Wright, 1956; Siller, 1976; Siller, Chipman, Ferguson, & Van, 1967). As a result, people with disabilities are often seen as having lower class status; are often underpaid for their employment; are more often relegated to sheltered workshops, even when they are able to accomplish tasks; have a very high unemployment rate (particularly in the case of women with disabilities) (Fine & Asch, 1988); often have fewer opportunities for higher education, especially with childhood-onset disabilities; are seen as asexual, incapable of parenting, or running a household; and are often physically abused.

The views of society are often reflected in the attitudes of others toward the person with the disability. Siller (1973) states, "Such terms as stigmatization, marginality, inferior status, [and] minority group position" (p. 473) are used when referring to the social psychological consequences of having a disability. Siller (1976), Siller et al. (1967), Yuker (1966), and Yuker et al. (1960) have done a great deal of work on attitudes toward those with disabilities and have constructed scales to measure those attitudes.

Siller (1973) found that attitudes toward people with disabilities were multidimensional in nature. He identified seven dimensions of importance in his attitudinal work, each of which may be necessary to look at when working with a client with a disability. His seven dimensions are:

1. interaction strain;
2. rejection of intimacy;

3. generalized rejection;
4. authoritarian virtuousness;
5. inferred emotional consequences;
6. distressed identification; and
7. imputed functional limitations (Siller, 1973).

Although most of the dimensions noted are easily understandable, 'authoritarian virtuousness' is not. Siller defines this dimension as "an ostensible 'pro-disabled' orientation which is rooted in an authoritarian context and advocates special treatment" (p. 475). Siller, however, sees this as a negative attitude toward disability covered by a misleading positive tone. Someone whose attitude toward disability is authoritarian virtuousness will treat a person with disability benevolently and altruistically, yet will not treat him as an equal. The individual with this type of attitude will vote to build a ramp at the local country club so that individuals with disabilities may gain access, and may even find the funding to do so, but will then make sure that no person with a disability is voted in as a member. The person with the authoritarian virtuousness attitude might invite people with disabilities to "special functions" at the newly ramped facility to demonstrate his benevolence; however, he would not invite those with disabilities to regular social functions at the same facility.

Beliefs held not only about people with disabilities, but sometimes *by* people with disabilities, are reflective of Siller's (1973) dimensions. Sweetland (1990) states that people with disabilities are often encouraged to hold irrational beliefs about their disabilities such that having a disability is itself viewed as catastrophic and awful. The converse perspective—i.e., that the disability presents no problems—also represents an irrational viewpoint. Sweetland (1990) states that another set of irrational beliefs held by those with disabilities is typified by the "universal fairness" principle: "Since bad things have happened to me, nothing bad should happen ever again, or I should now have an easy life to make up for my pain." A corollary belief, i.e., "The world owes me all good things because I have suffered enough," tends to reinforce the negative attitudes of the general society, which may view the person with a disability as dependent, angry, and unpleasant.

Although Siller touches upon some of the irrational attitudes of others toward those with physical disabilities, he does not discuss them in depth, nor does Sweetland. Dembo, Levitan and Wright (1956) and

Wright (1960) discussed the insider-outsider approach regarding those with disabilities. This is an approach characterized by an emphasis on difference rather than similarity. The outsiders (nondisabled) protect themselves from the fear of becoming disabled by focusing on the differences between themselves and people with disabilities. Wright (1960) emphasized the anormalization and salutary aspects of disability. This is a different, yet equally rejecting, way of viewing those with disabilities. It characterizes them as having superior powers and expresses admiration for their coping skills and achievements despite their disabilities. Although this view may appear complimentary to those with disabilities, like Siller's authoritarian virtuousness, it serves to maintain distance and difference, even though at first glance it seems to be positive.

This type of irrational view is a double-edged sword to those with disabilities. If they achieve only what is normally expected of others, they are rejected for not being special; if they are able to overachieve, they are considered too special to associate with others. This view may be so strongly held that unless an employee or student with a disability performs at a superior level at all times, he is seen as performing poorly. This can contribute to self-downing behavior and beliefs in those with disabilities, as well as downing of the person with the disability by others because they are not special.

The following section will discuss specific ways in which REBT is utilized when working with clients with disabilities. It will demonstrate that REBT techniques can be successfully used to deal with some of the attitudes and beliefs outlined above.

REBT WITH CLIENTS WITH DISABILITIES

Rational emotive behavior therapy (REBT) is uniquely suited for treating clients with disabilities. It is useful with any problems that might arise from the disability (i.e., the actual physical and performance limitations); with adjustment to the disability (e.g., new family arrangements, adjustments in work, and/or social interactions); and with other problems that may be complicated by the disability (such as dealing with family and co-workers' attitudes). Although some material has appeared in the REBT literature regarding the use of this therapeutic approach with persons having disabilities, much of it (Gandy, 1985, 1995; Sweetland, 1990) has been general in nature, and has not described specific intervention techniques. Gandy (1985, 1995) has been a proponent for the use of REBT by rehabilitation counselors when treating disability-related problems in a short-term setting, such as a rehabilitation facility. He has emphasized not only its appropriateness in brief interventional interaction, but also its value with a broad spectrum of clientele. REBT has been shown to be effective with clients from diverse cultural backgrounds, with clients from a broad spectrum of intelligence and educational levels, and with clients who have mental illnesses (Ellis, 1994a, 1994b). It is also an easy technique to implement and to teach to rehabilitation professionals. Regrettably, Gandy (1995) limits his case examples and his book to those people with disabilities who often seem to have cognitive impairments or low intelligence levels, and who are not really working on disability-related issues.

Calabro (1990) demonstrated the efficacy of REBT with patients with disabilities during the rehabilitation process. Sweetland (1990) discussed the irrational beliefs often held by parents of children with disabilities, as well as irrational beliefs that the person with the disability might hold. Rubin, Walen and Ellis (1990) discussed how to deal with irrational beliefs concerning diabetes and illness in general. Severe physical disability may, like diabetes, necessitate dealing with some uncomfortable realities. Coauthor Ellis (Rubin, Walen, and Ellis, 1990), who has had diabetes for many years, reminds therapists that core beliefs related to both ego anxiety and discomfort anxiety are best disputed philosophically. As described earlier, individuals with disabilities often have negative self-beliefs—reinforced by society, parents and employers—which may result in either feelings of personal inadequacy, or in anger regarding the way the world should be. According to Ellis, ego anxiety involves "self" beliefs and "entails perfectionistic and absolutistic demands for performance and/or approval to stave off feelings of severe inadequacy" (Rubin, Walen, and Ellis, p. 30). Discomfort anxiety results "when the world fails to arrange itself according to our equally absolutistic and perfectionistic demands for ease and comfort" (p. 30). The elegant solution, according to Ellis (1979), is to learn to accept the realities of diabetes and other chronic disabling conditions, and not awfulize about them. Ellis (1995) has stressed how he taught himself to stop whining about his various disabilities and to just get on with living and working toward his goals. He has indicated that he encourages his patients with disabilities to do the same. The various irrational beliefs that Rubin, Walen and Ellis discussed regarding diabetes can easily be extrapolated to most physical disabilities, and overlap those discussed by Calabro (1990) and Sweetland (1990). These irrational beliefs include the following:

1.   "It's not fair! Everyone else can eat what they want, why can't I? (So I will.)"
2.   "Doctors always sit there telling you what to do, and making you feel that you're a bad person for not doing everything they say. They don't have any idea how hard it is to live with diabetes. (So I won't go to see the doctor as often as I should.)"
3.   "If I go someplace unfamiliar for the weekend and I have a reaction, it'll be especially scary and I won't be able to stand it. (So I'll just stay home and feel depressed because my diabetes keeps me from doing things)" (Rubin, Walen, and Ellis, p. 29).

The issues encompassed by these beliefs (demands for fairness, the "need" to avoid disapproval, and "I-can't-stand-it-itis") often play a role in the emotional difficulties of those who are blind or visually impaired, deaf or hard of hearing, and those with orthopedic disabilities and learning disabilities.

One valuable and unique aspect of REBT is its sharing of information and use of bibliotherapy and educational materials (Rubin, Walen and Ellis, 1990). REBT therapists will sometimes discuss coping mechanisms they have used, that others have used, or that fictitious patients have used (Calabro, 1990) in order to deal with their difficulties. REBT therapists will often assign readings that not only deal with REBT techniques, but that are also more generally relevant to the problem the patient has. This type of assignment gives the client a sense of mastery and control—an issue very important to clients with disabilities.

SPECIAL CONSIDERATIONS FOR
REBT PRACTITIONERS

Although clients with disabilities will benefit from using rational emotive behavioral techniques in general, there are certain precautions and differences in approach that need to be noted by therapists.

Independence and Identity

Since many clients with disabilities have gone through rehabilitation in specialized short-term settings, they have been sensitized to being placed in a patient role. Many have found that one of the problems with the short-term facility is the loss of identity and status experienced by many clients. The client often begins the rehabilitation process as independent, but through staff attitudes and irrational beliefs is led to the cognitive distortion that she must now behave in a dependent manner in order to survive. This distortion is often accompanied by unexpressed anger.

When such a client comes for help with problem-solving, she may test the therapist to see if the same attitude is present as was encountered in the rehabilitation facility. This attitude may also imply to the client that not only has she lost a certain amount of physical functioning, but that the world now sees her as also having diminished cognitive functioning and less emotional stability. As one client succinctly put it, "Not only can I no longer walk, but now they're telling me that I've lost my mind as well."

Therefore, REBT counselors who work with clients with disabilities need to be aware of their own beliefs regarding disability. Dembo, Levitan, and Wright (1956) point out that therapists often use the insider-outsider attitude toward disabilities to allay their own fears about becoming disabled. Specifically, if they can find enough differences between themselves and their clients with disabilities, they do not have to face the threat that this "awful thing" (disability) could happen to them as well. This stance, however, distances the therapist from the client, and interferes with the way the client and therapist will work together. A lack of knowledge about disabling conditions may also reinforce this distance. Since everyone has irrational beliefs (Ellis, 1962), it is not unusual for therapists to hold such beliefs; however, it is harmful to the client if the therapist maintains this type of belief while working with a client with a disability.

If therapists are going to see clients with disabilities, it is advisable for them to examine their expectations, feelings and beliefs regarding such clients. It would be advisable for the therapist to picture the client as he or she expects that client to be, and ask the following:

1.   Have I prediagnosed the patient as being depressed, anxious, or helpless?

2. Do I have any pre-established prognosis for the patient (e.g., do I believe that the client will be difficult, unable to benefit from therapy, or have a poor prognosis)?

When examining feelings, the therapist can again picture the client as he or she is imagined and ask:

1. Do I feel pity for, anger with, or fear of the client?
2. Do I have feelings of disdain or superiority toward the client?

If any of these feelings or expectations are present, the therapist would most likely benefit from exploring his own beliefs regarding disability. Unhelpful beliefs may include:

"Having a disability would be awful or terrible"
"People with disabilities must not make waves"
"Having a disability is too much of an obstacle to overcome, and therefore all people with disabilities are depressed or severely disturbed" and
"People with disabilities are so inadequate and different that I (the therapist) could never relate to such a person."

If the therapist does find that he has any of these beliefs, they can hopefully be disputed. This disputation can be reinforced by asking the client with the disability more about the world she lives in. If the beliefs persist, it is probably not in the client's best interest for the therapist to continue seeing that client.

Heterogeneity of Disabilities

There are unique differences both between disabilities and within disabilities. As previously noted, people with the same disability may be more heterogeneous than homogeneous. Even if the therapist knows a great deal about disability—which is not often the case—she may not know the specifics of the person who has come for help. Therefore, it is often best not to make assumptions regarding the person with the disability, but instead to ask about the disability in an objective and respectful manner. Make the assumption at the outset that the client knows more about his specific disability than you do.

REBT therapists are uniquely trained to be nonauthoritarian in their therapy and to work in alliance with the client toward the client's goals. Therefore, REBT therapists are more open to the concept of allowing the patient to be an expert regarding self.

Self-Rating

Rational emotive behavior therapists make efforts to extend unconditional acceptance to their clients, and also attempt to directly teach them how to achieve a philosophy of self-acceptance. These features of REBT are of considerable importance when working with clients who have disabilities, as many of these individuals may engage in negative self-rating with respect to their disabilities. In addition, they will often have histories in which they have experienced nearly constant negative evaluations by other people. These other people may include significant figures such as parents and teachers (if disability onset was at birth or during childhood), employers, co-workers, and possibly spouses.

Ellis (1972, 1975) has indicated that the elegant solution to negative self-rating is to give up the self-created "need" to assign any sort of global rating of worth to oneself. Given the frequency with which clients with disabilities may experience negative evaluations by others, however, this elegant solution may represent a goal that they would have considerable difficulty in approaching. This difficulty may contribute to their becoming discouraged, which could have adverse effects on their progress in therapy. As an alternative, REBT therapists can teach these clients a less elegant, but still helpful, solution to the negative self-rating problem: Clients can accord worth to themselves simply because they are alive and possess some capacity to attain happiness and satisfaction (Ellis, 1972). The idea of having worth, despite limitations and possible performance decrement, would enhance life for the client with a disability more than would a battle for true unconditional self-acceptance in the face of so much nonacceptance in the wider world.

Supportive vs. Active-Directive Approaches

As Calabro (1990) pointed out, there are times when working with a person with a disability—especially during the rehabilitation process—when supportive, rather than confrontational, techniques are appropriate. The individual needs to assimilate new information slowly because of the overwhelming amount of change that he faces, and not be confronted with a reality that may be too difficult to be faced immediately. Calabro states that often, patients in active rehabilitation are not ready for active-directive approaches until near the time for discharge from the rehabilitation program. If the individual returns for counseling during outpatient treatment or after discharge, active disputing is useful, since the patient has had an opportunity to deal with the world with his disability and may now be ready to verbalize irrational beliefs.

Active listening and a supportive approach may also be needed when a client with a disability comes for psychotherapy. It allows the client with the disability to adapt to new situations and to see the therapist as a facilitator for change, rather than as another authority/expert who must be obeyed." A supportive stance during the first few sessions of psychotherapy also allows the therapist to see the patient's world through the patient's eyes. This world may be very different from that ever before experienced by the therapist. An active-directive stance with strong disputing becomes appropriate when the therapist has collected evidence of irrational beliefs (in the client's own words and across situations) regarding the world and others that are obviously interfering with the client's life.

Is the Client's Disability
the Presenting Problem?

One needs to remember when working with clients with disabilities that the disability is not always the problem. The client may present with relationship problems, work problems, or addiction problems, just as any other client might. It is best that the therapist avoid jumping to conclusions. If the therapist gathers evidence that points to a disability role in the problem, it is best to present this hypothesis socratically rather than presenting it from an expert viewpoint (i.e., "Is it possible that your disability may somehow impact this problem? If so, how do you see it having an effect?"). The therapist's assumptions about the role played by the disability may be at variance with what the client believes. If the therapist autocratically presents an inappropriate problem conceptualization, this might convey to the client that the therapist really has negative attitudes and beliefs both about the client and about disability.

Goal-Setting

It is wise, almost always, to let the client with the disability determine her own goals for therapy. Since the person with the disability may have learned to be dependent and may be resentful about the forced dependency, allowing the client to set the agenda is reinforcing and helpful in terms of re-establishing autonomy.

In traditional REBT, the client and therapist often either set goals together, or the client sets goals with the therapist's advice. The client with a disability, especially one who has gone through a rehabilitation experience, may be very cautious about contradicting the therapist, because the client has learned that to survive in the system it is best not to go against an authority figure. This stance may also lead the client to act in an especially suggestible manner, and to take the therapist's advice even when it is not what the client sees as appropriate. The therapist then becomes another authority figure in the client's life and the client with a disability may then leave therapy or not benefit from it.

Therapists can avoid this outcome by skillfully using questions that actively engage the client in the goal-setting process. For example: "You tell me that one of the problems that brings you here is a lack of assertiveness. What specifically would you like to work on regarding assertiveness and what would be your desired outcome?"

It may also be helpful to clarify client goals by asking situation-specific questions and relating these to the goal. For example, "Can you give me an example of a situation you've encountered where you thought that you weren't assertive enough? How would you have liked to change your responses in that situation if something similar occurred again?"

Actively Engaging the Client in Disputing Irrational Beliefs

Actively engage the client with a disability in the therapy process. Therapists dealing with a population of clients with disabilities are often tempted to lecture to such clients as a form of disputing irrational beliefs. This lecture style may be based on the therapist's own irrational beliefs regarding the capacity of a client with a disability to actively engage in disputing work due to a low energy level, imagined cognitive limitations, or stereotypical views of the client's helplessness.

Lecturing usually does not benefit the client. It does enforce a dramatic status difference between client and therapist, and sometimes will lead the client to withdraw from the therapy process. A more workable approach would be to begin teaching the client disputing techniques early in therapy through role-play situations.

Two types of role-playing are especially helpful. In the first, the client describes the situation and the therapist models disputing in the role of the client. In the second type of role-play, role reversal is used; the client is asked to act as therapist and teach the therapist (acting as the client) how to effectively dispute the irrational beliefs presented. The client (especially one who has a disability) benefits directly because approaching disputing in this way sends the message that the client is expected to be active, independent, and able to think things through. As therapy continues, the client with a disability can be encouraged to take direct responsibility for disputing with the therapist adding alternate ways of disputing that the client has not thought about ("Have you ever asked yourself . . .") Approaching disputing socratically with the client with a disability allows the client to agree or disagree with the therapist without surrendering autonomy or being wrong.

Bibliotherapy

The use of educational materials and outside resources (i.e., libraries and bookstores) is often helpful because this type of assignment indicates to the client that he is responsible for doing most of the work. The client is not there to be worked *on*, but rather worked *with*. Reading about REBT and about whatever topics may arise during therapy may indirectly bring forth irrational beliefs regarding being "special." This may occur because the client may state that he is too "special" to do the assignment and will not engage in it; or the materials chosen may in themselves bring the client to speak about beliefs about being "special or different." Other irrational beliefs regarding how society "should be" or regarding the fairness hypothesis may well emerge through the use of written materials.

Homework Consequences

It is necessary to check in advance on the potential consequences of attempting to effect change in particular client beliefs and behaviors.

One dramatic example of this is the client who came in and indicated to his therapist that he wanted more to do in his life. The therapist decided that he ought to go out and get a particular job as a data entry clerk. When the client stated that this would not be possible, the therapist assumed that the client had beliefs about being "too special to work," and attempted to push the client into a work setting. The client wisely refused and decided to terminate therapy. When the therapist asked the client why he was terminating therapy, the therapist was told that he was trying to put the client in a role where he would lose all of his medical benefits and the person who acted as his physical assistant (with personal hygiene, dressing, feeding, and transportation) and that he would therefore—with the small salary proposed—be unable to survive. Check with clients regarding the consequences of any homeworks or goals that may be established!

The following case description illustrates many of the problems presented by clients with disabilities, as well as some of the techniques used by REBT therapists to deal with these problems.

CASE ILLUSTRATION

In the case described below, a client with a disability (1) learned to accept her disability without negatively rating herself; (2) learned about the reality of her disability; (3) made progress in accommodating to the disability and with disputing irrational beliefs that were disability-related; and (4) worked on integrating her disability with its specific limitations into her lifestyle. Although certain therapeutic changes were difficult for her to make (particularly concerning irrational beliefs about herself and others) and these entailed some anger, this particular client succeeded in reaching her goals and managed to gain a happier and richer life than she had had previously. At the outset, it is important to note that therapy was made more difficult by the fact that the client's physical problems were as yet undiagnosed at the point she entered treatment. Consequently, she attributed the physical symptoms of her disabilities entirely to cognitive and emotional causes.

Introducing the Client

Helga, an attractive 40-year-old female, came to therapy because she "felt weaker and weaker and could not tolerate the idea of becoming more disabled." When she first came in she was well-dressed, slender, and carried an interestingly carved "walking stick," as she called it, which she immediately placed across the room from her seat and covered with her coat. She walked with a slight limp, which became more pronounced when she put her cane down. When asked about her walking, she responded that her limp was worse now because she had been exercising too much. She denied that the limp was a manifestation of her "weakness problem." Helga was the oldest of three children. She had one brother and one sister, neither of whom had any physical difficulties.

Helga stated that her physical "weakness" started just before she became a teenager. She remembered her parents taking her to her pediatrician and to the local hospital for evaluation. She stated, however, that she had not been told what (if anything) was wrong with her. Her family was very religious and depended heavily on their beliefs to get them through crises. Helga stated that she had been taught not to complain "no matter how bad she felt" or "how hard it was for her to get around." She stated that she had been taught that "a weakness of the mind leads to a weakness in the body," and that this was why she had come to therapy for help with her physical problems. She revealed upon further interview that she was also taught that a weak mind would not only impact her physically, but would also lead to a weak soul. To avoid this horrible result, she was told by her parents that she must never give in to her feelings, must never see herself as "handicapped" and must always work very, very hard to appear "normal." Her motto, which she repeated to herself many times a day was, "Appearing normal makes me normal."

Helga said that she was always taught that the worst thing that could happen to her would be for others—outsiders—to see her as her family saw her, i.e., as "weak and different." Her family had gone so far as to make a pledge that they would never reveal her weakness as long as she did not; therefore, no one need know "their horrible family secret." Helga stated that she had taken her mother's demands for normalcy very seriously, had tried very hard not to limp or appear weak, and had avoided becoming close to anyone outside the family so that others would not find out her "terrible secret." She also admitted that if she was ever tired or in pain (which was now occurring more often and had brought her to therapy) she would verbally "beat herself up for her shortcomings." She still, at the age of 40, had no idea of her physical diagnosis.

When asked how her weakness had impacted her life while she was growing up, she admitted only to being lonely. She stated that she had avoided sports and put all her energy into academics. She had very few friends as a child, and even those she had had lunch with at school were never invited to her home so that they would not know that anything was wrong with her. She also admitted that she had not dated in high school and had told her friends that it was because of her strong religious beliefs.

Helga said that she had attended a local college to which she could commute, so that she would not have to leave home. She also had attended graduate school while living at home. She had an MBA and worked as a managing director of publicity for a small publishing firm.

Helga finally left home and got her own apartment when she turned 33. She said that she had waited this long in order to afford a place of her own without needing a roommate "who might find out about her mental weakness."

Helga said that she was very frightened now because her weakness was impacting her work, which involved some travel and public presentations. She found that she was falling and limping more often than she had in the past. When she could no longer hide her symptoms, she told her co-workers that she had tried jogging and had hurt herself, and thus needed to use a walking stick for awhile.

When asked which physician she was seeing for her problem, Helga stared blankly ahead and repeated that if she were not weak and mentally deficient, she would have no need to be sitting in my office. She did not need a physician, but a doctor of the mind.

Initiating Therapy with Helga

Treatment with Helga began by teaching her the ABCs of REBT, emphasizing that it was not her physical condition per se that was causing her problem, but her beliefs about her situation. It was necessary to strongly present a reason for asking Helga to get her medical records so that a proper referral could be made as far as the type of medical specialist she would ultimately need to see. She was asked to contact her mother and anyone else who might be able to give her information. Helga reluctantly accepted the assignment, but was unable to overcome the strength of her mother's projected reply, which was that it was all in Helga's head. Since Helga's belief—that her physical problems were all due to being emotionally weak and damaged—was so strong, she was asked for evidence to back her belief. The evidence was to be supplied in two forms, one form being a journal which she was to keep of her medical symptoms, and her ABCs when they occurred, and the second form being research which she would do at the local medical library.

Encountering Obstacles to Therapy

Helga had a great deal of difficulty doing the latter assignment, which we agreed would last a month. She reported that when she tried to even picture herself looking at any type of book concerning muscular weakness, she became very anxious. During this first month, we worked on her ABCs, which allowed her to strongly see that her belief system, not her weakness, was at the root of her anxiety. After three sessions of relaxation breathing, desensitization, and learning the basics of REBT, Helga was able to verbalize the following beliefs regarding disability and her fear of admitting to having a disability:

   1.   If I am disabled, it is because I have sinned and am being punished for my sins . . . and I couldn't stand having to live with that thought.
   2.   A weak body is the result of a weak mind.
   3.   Having a physical disability is about the worst thing that could happen to anyone and is truly awful.
   4.   No one could ever love any human who is physically imperfect, and therefore I am truly unlovable.
   5.   It would be a catastrophe if I let my parents down by admitting to having a disability.

Since Helga had held these beliefs since childhood, during the first few weeks of therapy, she could not see how these beliefs could ever change. She stated that she felt saddled with them and doomed to keep them for the rest of her life. She did, however, agree to keep recording her symptoms. We agreed to suspend the library part of the assignment until she had learned to dispute her beliefs more strongly.

Disputing Beliefs

As Helga recorded her symptoms in her journal, she found that both her symptoms and her beliefs followed a pattern. She would awaken fairly refreshed, but often stiff in the morning, and she noted that her gait and the way she walked was fairly constant; that is, her gait pattern did not change. She would tire during the day, even though she was cognitively alert, and by evening she would often lose her balance and need to rely more on her cane. She found that she would wake up with the belief that "If I don't think about my body, and concentrate on being a good Christian, my disability will go away." However, later in the day as she tired, she would immediately put herself down for failing and become depressed, morose, and then angry. She would then focus on most of the beliefs listed above.

After she had generated the list and the pattern, she was asked how this pattern of tiring, limping, emotionally beating herself up, self-downing, and catastrophizing was helpful to her. She was finally able to see that her beliefs were only making her miserable. When asked how she would treat others with disabilities, she said that she would avoid them because they were obviously "weak sinners" like she was. This was the opening that was needed to challenge her belief. She was given the homework assignment of reading about famous people, both past and present, with disabilities such as Franklin Delano Roosevelt, Helen Keller, and Itzhak Perlman. She was then asked to comment on whether she would have liked to have been personally acquainted with these people.

Since Helga was very intelligent, she was able to generate quite a long list of celebrities past and present with disabilities, and found that she would have really enjoyed having a friendship with many of these famous people whom she really admired. She also found that all of the disabilities she read about had causes that could not be controlled by the individual with the disability. She was even able to see that her disability might have a cause over which she had no control. At this point she decided that she would like to try disputing her beliefs.

We began Helga's disputes by using thought-stopping procedures wherein she would substitute a rational statement for her negative irrational beliefs. As soon as she began her usual downward spiraling pattern, she would snap the rubber band which she had been instructed to wear around her wrist and subvocally say "STOP!" She would then tell herself strongly that "having a physical limitation is neither pleasant nor convenient, but it is not a catastrophe." After employing the rational belief for a week, Helga reported that her self-downing had markedly decreased. She was finally able to discuss her physical symptoms honestly and objectively and even to speculate that they had a physical rather than an emotional cause.

Obtaining a Physical Diagnosis

The next step in therapy was very difficult for Helga, and she began canceling sessions in order to avoid the inevitable; however, since her symptoms were not improving, she decided that she needed to come in again. This step, which Helga saw as horrifying, was to seek medical help to assist her in trying to find the cause of her physical problems.

Helga stated that she had only seen physicians for pre-employment checkups and had used the employee health service only for treatment of colds and other unavoidable minor ailments. Aside from her weakness and strange gait, she reported being in very good health. She stated that pre-employment medical examinations had been pro forma and it had been easy to tell the physicians that everything was fine except for the "pulled muscle and limp which I always told them was from jogging." She also realized that it would be wise to try to get her medical history from her parents, before making a physician's appointment.

We role-played Helga's asking her parents for information. She found the idea of dealing with this "taboo topic" with them to be highly anxiety inducing for her. She rehearsed for two weeks, relying heavily on rational coping statements and relaxation techniques, in order to be able to confront them. She imagined them turning their backs to her and throwing her out of the house. She was able to realize that she would probably get a negative reaction for raising the topic of her weakness. She practiced telling herself that she could not force her parents to tell her anything, and that she did not have to take it personally if they refused. She also practiced imagining "the worst possible scenario," which she described as having her parents accuse her of being "crazy," turning their backs to her as they "prayed for her soul," and asking her to "not come home again because of the depth of her sinning." When asked how possible this scenario was, she reluctantly said that it had a 30% possibility of occurring and that she had to be prepared in case it did happen.

Finally, she did approach her parents. She reported back that although they had not thrown her out of the house, they had refused to give her the information that she sought, including the name of the hospital they had taken her to when ill. They claimed that it had no bearing on her life and that it would be useless to her. They also told her that they would pray for her because her soul was obviously in turmoil. Helga said that her parents had acted kindly toward her, but had stated that they "had her best interests at heart and knew that she would be better off forgetting all about it."

When asked what Helga thought she should do next considering all the evidence accruing in her symptom log, she reluctantly agreed that it was time to seek medical advice. She found this frightening, and when asked if she could have her gynecologist give her a referral to a good internist, she became very embarrassed and admitted that she had never seen a gynecologist. Her mother had told her, when she was a young adult, that "with no man in her life, she would never have to worry about those types of problems." She did, however, have a friend from college who was a nurse and could advise her. She was, by this point, able to generate an anti-anxiety coping statement for herself, which was: "Making an appointment with a physician makes me normal, not abnormal, and if other normal people can tolerate it, so can I."

Helga luckily found a knowledgeable internist who sent her to a neurologist for further evaluation. She was diagnosed as having Charcot-Marie-Tooth Syndrome, a neurological condition which usually has an onset somewhere between mid-childhood and age 30. She was told that it was slowly degenerative, but that the symptoms could stop getting worse and remain stable. Once she was given a diagnosis, Helga was able to do research on the problem, and was finally reassured that sin and mental weakness bore no connection to her physical difficulties. She was referred to a physiatrist for evaluation and treatment of her gait problem. She was sent for bracing and physical therapy and was taught how to hide the brace if she so chose.

Dealing with Anger

Surprisingly, rather than depressing Helga, the diagnosis inspired her to more vigorously dispute the irrational beliefs that she had held since childhood. The medical evidence she had acquired finally gave her the strength to absolve herself of what she had believed were her spiritual and emotional deficiencies. This, however, led to more problems for Helga. She found that she was furious with her parents for "robbing her of a normal adolescence," as well as "lying to her and making her feel deficient." She stated that she wanted to "vent all her anger at them and let them see what they had done to her." When asked what the consequences of these actions would be, she said she didn't know, but she was nevertheless determined that her parents should ask for her forgiveness, instead of her asking for theirs.

Helga was given the homework of imagining the scene she so dearly desired and imagining it repeatedly and strongly. She was then told to list all the possible consequences—both positive and negative—of having such a confrontation. She was also to imagine both the best and worst possible outcomes, and to rate the likelihood of each. This homework helped Helga realize that the probability of her having the outcome she desired was negligible, and that the more likely result would be that her parents would be shocked and hurt and not relate to her at all. She decided that she would tell them about her diagnosis and how she felt about it, in an assertive, but not hostile, fashion. She would also tell them that she was angry with them for not getting her the help she needed when the physical problem was first diagnosed, and what she believed the consequences had been for her of not getting that help. She also realized that if she were too condemnatory in her presentation, she might meet with rejection. She again was able to create a coping statement to help her, which was: "I am ready to change; however, that does not mean that my parents will change. I can only change my own beliefs and behavior. I cannot force anyone else to change, unless they want to change." She also told herself, "If my parents cannot understand or accept what I am saying, it will be sad for me, but I can tolerate it."

Helga reported back that she had calmly told her parents what had happened and that she now used both braces and a cane which facilitated her walking. She further reported that she found these aids helpful because she did not tire as easily or lose her balance as much as she had in the past. She also related that she really regretted the fact that her parents had not gotten her help sooner. She stated that they were shocked and unwilling to accept what she had done, and said that they'd rather she hid "the ugly truth about herself." Helga said that the outcome was not what she had hoped for, but that it had been valuable because she could see that the "ideological problem was now theirs and not mine." She stated that she would still prefer not to have a physical disability; however, since she did have Charcot-Marie-Tooth, she was ready to learn how to really live with it.

Making Life Changes

Helga decided that she wanted to change what had been her life. She wanted to become involved with people her own age. She wanted to socialize and she wanted to begin dating. She now understood that whether she hid her physical disability or did not, it would still be there, and she would still have to cope with it. She decided to take a workshop in social skills training. She also worked at constructing assignments for herself that would force her to begin to socialize with others, such as signing up for a class in photography and joining a church singles' group, which had regular meetings and went on trips together. She contacted her physical therapist and asked whether she could be taught some form of ballroom dancing. The physical therapist agreed to work on this with her and to explore other physical activities she might be able to engage in with the group.

Helga's only other problems that needed to be addressed before leaving therapy were how to handle needing a cane and how to deal with disappointments if certain people in her life, or who were to be in her life, would not or could not accept her limitations. Helga knew that since she was not allowed to jog and did not want to lie, she could no longer attribute the cane to sports accidents. She was able to use the technique of reframing to deal with the issue of the cane. She was able to view her cane as something that assisted her and added to her efficiency, rather than as detrimental and detracting from her. Since she needed evidence to support this belief, she took a weekend day and did not use the cane. She found that she tired more quickly and that her mobility was quite limited.

Terminating Therapy

Helga decided after 20 sessions that she was ready to terminate therapy. I told her that this was fine, but that I wanted her to check in by either phone or letter 3 months from the time of our last session.

After 3 months, she decided to come in for two sessions devoted to both disability-related problems and nondisability-related problems.

One of these sessions was informational in nature and was devoted to methods she could use to deal with the attitudes of others she had met in her "new life" regarding her disability. She had a difficult time in understanding their irrational beliefs, since she was disabled and they were not. She agreed to read some of the attitude toward disability research that had been conducted, and concluded that it was sad that people could have such "weird ideas regarding a physical condition." She laughed when reminded that she once possessed that type of "weird idea" herself before she had learned good reality-testing and disputing techniques and reframing.

The second session was devoted to discussion of some of the new behaviors Helga was now engaged in and how to handle novel situations. The "new behavior" that Helga referred to was dating, and the problems she presented in this area had no relation to her disability. Helga stayed in contact and continued to make progress. She reported some disappointments, but in general that she was doing well, and maintaining a steady relationship with a man for the first time in her life.

Case Summary

The case of Helga illustrates many of the REBT principles that are successfully used with clients with disabilities. Her disability originated in childhood and she had learned to imbibe her parents' attitudes concerning the disability. The cost of not doing so would have been parental rejection. Instead of damning her parents, however, Helga took the lead in deciding how she wanted to handle her problem. She was intelligent, as are many people with disabilities. Many learn to develop their cognitive skills because these are often not affected by the physical disability, and developing them gives them a sense of mastery that would not be possible when trying to manage unchangeable physical limitations.

Helga had been able to establish an independent, yet rather unfulfilling, life because of the irrational beliefs she clung to and refused to relinquish. The cost of relinquishing her beliefs without an alternative—i.e., losing her parents' love and support—was too high for her to pay immediately. Since she had little outside social contact when she entered therapy, she needed to take her time and carefully look at the long-term consequences of her actions.

Helga was able to make dramatic changes in her life because she controlled the speed at which change was made and was able to weigh the consequences of each action she decided to take. Even though therapy was often difficult for her, she knew that she was respected and that she was in control. Helga, like many clients with disabilities, had negative views regarding disabilities, as well as irrational views regarding having a disability. These views needed to change before she could change. Helga's case points out that when changing firmly held beliefs, it is often best to go to a rational coping statement, rather than immediately reframing the situation in a positive light which will only be superficially believed by the client.

Helga's case also illustrates the importance of the therapist's remaining objective. If the therapist tends to take the client's "side" in certain situations and acts as an advocate, the client may blame the therapist for later consequences of actions taken.

Helga's case had a very positive outcome. This will not always be true with clients with disabilities, no more than in any other patient population. It is wise when working with clients with disabilities to always check on both the short- and long-term consequences of projected solutions.

CONCLUSION

REBT is especially appropriate for treating clients with disabilities. REBT's strengths include the therapist's acceptance of each client as unique, with his or her own strengths and weaknesses; valuing each client for himself or herself; listening to the client's view of the world nonjudgmentally and allowing the client to collect evidence to prove these views; reinforcing reality without judging the client; and finding and disputing irrational beliefs about an irrational world. For some clients with disabilities, learning high frustration tolerance and giving up the "fair world" hypothesis may lead to more adaptive ways of viewing the world and finding happiness. REBT's focus on helping the client learn new skills, as well as disputing irrational ways of viewing the world, can be most helpful for this client population.

REFERENCES

Americans with Disabilities Act of 1990, 42 U.S.C.A. § 12101 *et seq.* (West 1993).

Calabro, L. (1990). Adjustment to disability: A cognitive behavioral model for analysis and clinical management. *Journal of Rational-Emotive and Cognitive Behavior Therapy, 8,* 79–103.

Dembo, T., Levitan, G., & Wright, B. (1956). Adjustment to misfortune: A problem of social psychological rehabilitation. *Artificial Limbs, 3,* 4–62.

Dorge, C. A. (Ed.) (1995). *The statistical record of health and medicine.* New York: International Thomson.

Ellis, A. (1962). *Reason and emotion in psychotherapy.* Secaucus, NJ: Citadel.

Ellis, A. (1972). *Psychotherapy and the value of a human being.* New York: Institute for Rational-Emotive Therapy.

Ellis, A. (1975). *RET abolishes most of the human ego.* New York: Institute for Rational-Emotive Therapy.

Ellis, A. (1979). Discomfort anxiety: A new cognitive-behavioral construct. Part I. *Rational Living, 14,* 3–8.

Ellis, A. (1994a). Rational emotive behavior therapy approaches to obsessive-compulsive disorder (OCD). *Journal of Rational-Emotive & Cognitive-Behavior Therapy, 12,* 121–141.

Ellis, A. (1994b). The treatment of borderline personalities with rational emotive behavior therapy. *Journal of Rational-Emotive & Cognitive-Behavior Therapy, 12,* 101–119.

Ellis, A. (1995, August). Using rational emotive behavioral techniques to cope with disability. Invited Address given at the 103rd Annual Convention of the American Psychological Association, New York, NY.

Fine, M., & Asch, A. (1988). *Women with disabilities: Essays in psychology, culture, and politics.* Philadelphia: Temple University Press.

Gandy, G. L. (1985). Frequent misperceptions of rational-emotive therapy: An overview for the rehabilitation counselor. *Journal of Applied Rehabilitation Counseling, 16,* 31–35.

Gandy, G. L. (1995). *Mental health rehabilitation: Disputing irrational beliefs.* Springfield, IL: Charles C. Thomas.

Martin, S. (1995). Are children with disabilities more likely to be abused? *The APA Monitor, 26*(10), 48.

Rubin, R., Walen, S., & Ellis, A. (1990). Living with diabetes. *Journal of Rational-Emotive & Cognitive-Behavior Therapy, 8*(1), 21–39.

Shontz, F. C. (1975). *The psychological aspects of physical illness and disability.* New York: Macmillan.

Siller, J. (1973). Psychosocial aspects of physical disability. In J. Meislin (Ed.), *Rehabilitation medicine and psychiatry* (pp. 455–484). Springfield, IL: Charles C. Thomas.

Siller, J. (1976). Attitudes toward disability. In H. Rusalem & D. Malikin (Eds.), *Contemporary vocational rehabilitation* (pp. 67–80). New York: New York University Press.

Siller, J., Chipman, A., Ferguson, L. T., & Van, D. H. (1967). *Studies in reactions to disability: XI Attitude of the non-disabled toward the physically disabled.* New York: New York University Press.

Sweetland, J. D. (1990). Cognitive-behavior therapy and physical disability. *Journal of Rational-Emotive & Cognitive-Behavior Therapy, 8*(2), 71–78.

U.S. Department of Commerce. (1995). *The statistical abstract of the United States: The national data book* (114th ed.). Washington, DC: Author.

Wright, B. A. (1960). *Physical disability: A psychological approach.* New York: Harper & Row.

Yuker, H. E., Block, J. R., & Campbell, W. J. (1960). *A scale to measure attitudes toward disabled persons.* Albertson, NY: Human Resources Press.

Yuker, H. E. (1966). *The measurement of attitudes toward disabled persons.* Albertson, NY: Human Resources Press.

CHAPTER 5

Rational-Emotive Family Therapy

Charles H. Huber

As a family psychologist, the family systems perspective represents the guiding core of my research and clinical practice with Rational-Emotive Family Therapy (REFT). Although the family is the primary unit of focus and analysis in REFT, it is not the only significant system of influence. REFT also considers the interconnections and simultaneous interaction of multiple systems of influence, including the psychological world of the individual as well as his or her biological, social, cultural, spiritual, political, and economic environments. The *family systems perspective* and especially *family beliefs,* however, are the predominant emphases of REFT assessment, intervention, and evaluation.

THE FAMILY AS A SYSTEM

Traditionally, human interactions have been looked at as being connected in a straight line such that one element of an interaction (A) leads to the next element (B) and so forth (A→ B→ C→ . . .). The family systems perspective breaks with this traditional linear view and posits the concept of *circular causality.* Circular causality conceives of every element of an interaction as being part of a sequence of simultaneous interactions that are all interconnected. This is illustrated in Figure 5.1.

Linear causality.
A influences B, but B does not influence A.
"I treat you like a child because you behave like a
child."
"I behave like a child because you treat me like a
child."

A ────────────────▶ B

Circularity
A and B are in dynamic interaction.

"When I treat you like a child, you behave like a
child, and then I treat you like a child even more
and you behave even more like a child. We sure
have a vicious cycle going, don't we?"

"When I behave like a child, you treat me like a
child, and then I behave like a child even more.
We are sure caught up with each other, aren't we?"

Figure 5.1   Linear and circular causality.
Note: From *Equilibrium family therapy: A basic guide for the helping professions*
(p. 44), by C. H. Huber & P. A. Driskill, 1993. New York: Crossroad. Copyright
1993 by Crossroad. Reprinted by permission.

Figure 5.1 shows a sequence of continuous interaction with no
beginning and no end. How any interactional sequence is viewed,
therefore, depends upon where the viewer chooses to place the primary emphasis.

Consider, for example, a family at dinner with a small child who is
not eating, and two parents who believe it is essential for the child to
eat a "good" dinner. A traditional linear position would suggest that
the child is not a "good" eater, so the parents believe they must take
action to ensure that the child eats. Taking a family systems perspective
incorporating circular causality contributes to a view of this interaction that is much broader. The child does not eat immediately, leading

to the parents thinking they must demand that the child eat, leading to the child crying and even eating less, leading to more parental demands. The same interaction could just as easily begin, however, with the parents thinking they must push the child to eat as soon as dinner begins, leading to the child feeling pressured and not eating, leading to more parental pushing, leading to greater pressure experienced by the child and consequently even less eating, and so on.

A traditional linear position focuses singularly on that portion of the interaction in which the child is not eating and the parents are thinking that they need to encourage eating behavior; it suggests that the child is either not hungry, or is destructively oppositional. A contrasting linear view might begin with the parents thinking that they need to push the child to eat and the child then not eating, and suggests that the parents are thinking and then acting in a destructively demanding manner.

Viewing the entire interaction in a circular manner without attempting to establish a linear cause and effect is the family systems perspective. All parts of the interaction are equally attended to. Instead of seeing the "problem" as either the child not eating or the parents thinking they need to be pushy, it is seen as "both-and." The mutual, simultaneous interaction of the child and parents cannot be separated. Neither alone is the "problem." *Both* the child *and* the parents together, *how they simultaneously interact with each other,* constitute the "problem."

The family systems perspective posits that treatment can arbitrarily begin at any point in an interactional sequence. Returning to the above example, a therapist could look to facilitate change on the part of the parents or child—preferably both—that encourages the child to begin eating or the parents to think in a more reasonable way—again, preferably both—and to facilitate change to the extent that the child increases the amount of food ingested and the parents think more reasonably.

That portion of the interactional sequence where REFT chooses to primarily target and focus change efforts is the family's common belief about any difficulty they encounter. It is important to stress again, however, that REFT takes a family systems position: that both the difficulty and the family belief occur simultaneously, and it is a systemically arbitrary choice to select family beliefs as the primary target and focus for change efforts. This will be addressed further in later discussion on the ABCs of REFT.

FAMILY BELIEFS

Families are belief-governed systems; their members behave among themselves in an organized, repetitive manner, and from this patterning of behaviors can be abstracted governing principles of family life (Jackson, 1977). These beliefs thus represent the norms that direct behavior within the family system.

Most family beliefs are unwritten and operate covertly. Initially, they first develop as simple *inferences* that all family members make relative to the repetitive patterns of interaction they observe occurring around them. "Father does the grocery shopping; mother does the cooking." "Child A is a fine student; Child B is a marginal student. Child B, however, is an athlete; Child A is not interested in athletics." "We go to the 11:00 A.M. church service every Sunday." A typical family belief, at the inference level, unstated but understood by all, is that major decisions are made by parents and handed down to children.

These family beliefs at the inference level are *non-evaluative,* that is, they are simple statements of fact or presumed fact. REFT emphasizes the importance of addressing family beliefs as *evaluations;* that being the degree to which family members appraise or evaluate something as desirable or undesirable (Wessler & Wessler, 1980). Consider below, for example, a newly married couple who came from families in which conflict was dealt with quite differently.

Open discussion of problems and accompanying feelings of anger or frustration were always encouraged in Betsy's family. She, her parents, and siblings would often get into loud shouting matches. They were able, however, to adequately resolve their differences in this manner and often joked in the aftermath of such problem-solving sessions about their seemingly volatile interactions. Charles' family, by contrast, valued calm, deliberate problem-solving. When expressions of anger or hurt feelings arose, family members would withdraw to themselves until they were able to come together again in a calmer manner and resolve their differences. Prior to marrying, few significant difficulties were experienced by Betsy and Charles. A year into their marriage, however, Charles' withdrawal and Betsy's open expression of anger became a vicious cycle of increasingly greater withdrawal and more intense angry feelings exhibited by each respectively.

Whenever difficulties arose, Betsy and Charles each maintained their own individual beliefs learned in their families of origin. At the inference level, their "common" family belief, unconsciously followed by them and applied to themselves, was "We handle difficulties the way they were handled in our parents' home." Unfortunately, at the evaluation level, the rigidity ("We *must* . . .") with which they *demanded* adherence to this common family belief contributed to increasing discord between them. The more Betsy expressed her anger, the more Charles withdrew; the more he withdrew, the more she expressed her anger.

REFT stresses the role played by *rational* and *irrational* family beliefs with respect to family functioning. Rational family beliefs are those that have personal significance for family members and that *evaluate* situations in an adaptive, helpful manner. By "personal significance" is meant a belief of importance to family members, and not simply a passing thought (e.g., "Family loyalty is an important value for us," versus "What a pretty day").

Rational family beliefs are also relative in nature. There is no set right or wrong, but rather, consideration is given to every situation as unique and potentially calling for a different response. When families are able to think about their circumstances in a relative manner, they are more likely to experience feelings that indicate pleasure; sometimes they also experience feelings that indicate displeasure, such as sadness, annoyance, and concern. Although these latter emotions are not necessarily pleasurable, they are considered appropriate responses if the circumstances encountered are negative; they do not significantly interfere with the family's pursuit of desired goals or, if these goals are forever blocked, the selection and pursuit of new goals. These "helpful" feelings (relative to the circumstances encountered) accompany rational family beliefs, which are nonabsolute, adaptive statements of personal significance (Dryden, 1984).

Irrational family beliefs are those that have personal significance for family members and are stated in an absolute, unhelpful manner. Feelings accompanying irrational beliefs include expressions of depression, anger, and guilt. These expressions of "hurtful" emotions are seen as going hand in hand with exaggerated *evaluations* of situations and thus are maladaptive to even very negative circumstances because they generally impede the pursuit of family goals.

Family beliefs and the degree of rationality-irrationality characterizing them are the primary focus of REFT. Until Betsy and Charles are able to move to a more relative and thus rational position with regard to their rigidly held common family belief, significant discord will very likely continue in their relationship. For example, from "We must handle difficulties the way they were handled in our parents' home," movement might be facilitated toward "We can try to (i.e., "we don't *have to*") handle difficulties the way they were handled in our parents' home, but we can also look for our own (i.e., "new and/ or different") ways as well."

"Rationality" characterizes adaptive family beliefs, and thus optimal family functioning. The more family interactions are characterized by a philosophy of rationality within a family system, the more readily that system is able to be open to, and assimilate new information so as to either maintain or change its beliefs as it evolves in its life cycle development.

PROBLEM CONCEPTUALIZATION

All families encounter expected as well as unexpected life difficulties. REFT views recurring difficulties as a consequence of families responding in absolutist and/or exaggerated (i.e., irrational) ways. When the same difficulties continuously recur within a family system, a predominance of absolutist and/or exaggerated family beliefs accompanies the ineffective solutions employed by family members to diffuse the impact of the difficulties they are encountering. Fisch, Weakland, and Segal (1982) offered insight as to the logic of this common occurrence:

> But why would anyone persist in attempting solutions that do not work and, indeed, often make things progressively worse? . . . [W]e explain the persistence of unproductive behavior on the basis of a few simple observations involving a minimum of inference and theoretical constructs: (1) From early in life, we all learn culturally standard solutions for culturally defined problems. These standard solutions often work, but sometimes they do not. Since they have been learned largely at an unconscious or implicit level, to question or alter such solutions is very difficult. (2) When people are in stressful situations, as they are when struggling with problems, their behavior usually becomes *more* constricted and rigid. (3) Contrary to the widespread view that people are illogical, we propose that people are *too* logical; that is they act logically in terms of basic, unquestioned premises, and when undesired results occur, they

employ further logical operations to explain away the discrepancy, rather than revising the premises. (p. 287).

REFT maintains a solution focus relative to the specifics of problem conceptualization. Thus, for expected as well as unexpected life difficulties to become problems (a problem being defined as a recurring difficulty that has proven resistant to attempts to resolve it), the difficulty is made worse by employing poor problem-solving strategies (i.e., unsuccessful solutions). The majority of these solutions are not necessarily unsuccessful in and of themselves, but rather represent either an exaggeration or denial of the dynamics of a family's experience. *Taking the position of circular causality and although still arbitrary from a family systems perspective, REFT (emanating from rational-emotive theory) pragmatically posits the single overarching principle of problem conceptualization as being the predominance of unsuccessful solutions accompanied by absolutist and/or exaggerated family beliefs.* Ellis (1993) referred to this as "the primacy of absolutist shoulds and musts" (p. 6). He stated further in this regard:

> RET assumes, in other words, that you are often a profound musturbator and that once you strongly construct absolutist *musts* and *must nots* you will very easily and often, when you, others, and the world contradict them, slide yourself into "logical" but misleading inferences that "confirm" and add to your disturbed reactions. . . . RET's cardinal rule when people are thinking, feeling, and acting neurotically is "Cherchez le should! Cherchez le must! Look for the should! Look for the must!" RET assumes that people with disturbance overtly and/or tacitly have one, two, or three underlying musts, that these can usually be quickly found, and then actively and forcefully Disputed and changed back to preferences. (Ellis, 1993, p. 8)

ASSESSMENT: THE ABC'S OF REFT

As an overarching principle, REFT maintains the importance of assessment throughout the course of therapy. Treatment should begin with adequate assessment and be consistently monitored relative to that assessment, and evaluation procedures be conducted as a component of termination in order to provide meaningful outcome data.

The work of REFT thus begins by assessing family ABCs: The cognitive, emotive, and behavioral frames of reference family members experience relative to the concerns being presented for treatment. Assessing these frames of reference is an ongoing process, done continuously as the therapeutic process proceeds. Its purpose is to understand what is occurring within a family so as to make suitable interventions, both at the onset of treatment and subsequently. Before describing the procedures involved in assessing family frames of reference within REFT, it is prudent to offer several prefacing remarks in order to place the REFT assessment process into proper perspective.

REFT takes a family systems position advocating circular causality: that is, every element of an interaction is part of a sequence of simultaneous interactions that are all interconnected. This basic assumption, again, is critical to keep in mind, particularly in considering the REFT concepts of "exception times" and A'B'C' that will now be presented. Recall that REFT (emanating from rational-emotive theory) pragmatically posits that "problems" are conceptualized as being *unsuccessful solutions accompanied by absolutist and/or exaggerated family beliefs.* Also accompanying these REFT "problems" are typically distressful and unsatisfying emotions and behaviors.

Families involved in unresolved conflicts tend to become stereotyped in the repetitive mishandling of these conflicts, with the result that they narrow observations of their circumstances to focus primarily on the conflict. Consequently, they regard their more competent ways of functioning as disassociated from their conflict circumstances. When most families present for therapy, they assert the more dysfunctional aspects of their interactions; these they perceive to be the areas most relevant to treatment. These dysfunctional aspects of families' presentations are assessed according to a traditional ABC assessment applied to families: A = Activating Event; B = Family Belief; C = Emotional and Behavioral Consequences. REFT takes the ABCs one further step to A', B', C' (which is read A–prime, B–prime, and C–prime). A'B'C' represents the Activating Event (A'), Family Belief (B'), and Emotional and Behavioral Consequences (C') of competent ways that families have functioned; however, for reasons unknown, they have tended to disassociate these competent ways from their conflict circumstances. Note that in this conceptualization, A and A' are not regarded as events that serve to "trigger" beliefs which then lead to particular emotional and behavioral consequences. This "triggering" view would be part of the traditional linear paradigm for understanding human interactions. Rather, in keeping with the family systems perspective of viewing the elements of interactions as mutual and simultaneous, A and A′ are viewed as simply *accompanying* family beliefs and emotional and behavioral consequences.

REFT recognizes that families' presentations of dysfunctional interactions represent only one segment of their total functioning. No matter what the intensity or duration of the difficulties families experience, there are always situations or times when, for some reason, the difficulty is handled well (O'Hanlon & Weiner-Davis, 1989). Parents feel comfortable trusting their rebellious adolescents, adolescents perceive their parents' rules to be reasonable, combative couples spend an enjoyable evening together, etc. Most families, however, consider these less difficult or difficulty-free times unrelated to those times when the difficulty is fully felt in all its pain and discomfort, so little is done to better understand or amplify these better functioning times.

Most therapists are trained to be enthusiastic psychopathologists. Were they to expand their focus of assessment, they would find that all families already have the skills and resources to resolve their presenting complaints. As Ellis (1987) posited of all human beings:

> Their very nature is, first, to have probabilities and realistic expectations, and hopes of fulfilling their goals and wishes, and to feel appropriately sad, sorry, displeased, and frustrated when these are not met. But, being somewhat allergic to probability . . . when they have strong and paramount desires they very frequently, and often unconsciously or implicitly, escalate their longings into unconditional and rigid insistencies and commands. (p. 373)

The REFT therapist recognizes that all families will likely at some time have rational as well as irrational family beliefs about their circumstances. It is the role of the therapist to assist families in recognizing their rational family beliefs (as well as their irrational family beliefs) and put them to greater use. REFT therapists do not attempt to have families "reinvent the wheel." They, instead, look to put readily available "spare tires" to much greater use.

There are almost always "exception times." Exception times occur whenever a difficulty is being adequately dealt with. Successful solutions are a part of the repertoire of all families; most just don't realize it. They say to themselves, "We must employ solution A or fail." For whatever reason, solution A seems to them to be the right (logical, best, only) choice. As a result, other alternatives are lumped together and excluded. Were families experiencing conflict to expand their perspective, they would see that they already possess the skills and resources to resolve their problems (de Shazer et al., 1986). Assessing the dynamics of one or more exception times relating to a family's presenting concern represents the A'B'C' of REFT.

Following from the above, assessment to provide data relative to the more specific aspects of treatment planning begins and continues throughout therapy. The initial focus of the assessment is to generate information gathering relative to: (1) the nature of the family's complaint (unsuccessful solutions, reframed as desired goals) and how the complaint is generally being unsuccessfully addressed [A]; (2) the common family belief accompanying the unsuccessful solution and the degree of rationality-irrationality characterizing that belief [B]; and (3) the emotional and behavioral consequences also accompanying A and B [C]. Assessment then moves to (4) a detailed description of a successful solution employed by the family during a time they were functioning in a more competent manner in similar circumstances [A' of the exception time]; (5) the typically more rational family belief accompanying the successful solution of the exception time [B']; and (6) the emotional and behavioral consequences also accompanying A' and B' [C'] as the family functioned in a more competent manner during the exception time.

The ABC analysis represents an illustration of the family's dominant dilemma, while the latter A'B'C' analysis offers an example of the earlier mentioned "spare tire" relative to the family's overall functioning. These two analyses later become the foci for therapeutic intervention during the Debate process (D) of REFT.

Complaints as Goals

REFT considers early assessment of family members' expectations for therapy as critical, given that positive expectancy increases the likelihood of positive therapeutic effect, whereas incongruence between or among family members' and therapist expectations for the process significantly decreases therapeutic efficacy. Thus, presenting concerns are quickly tied to goals, the attainment of which the family would see as alleviating their presenting complaint (i.e., "In sharing with me the concerns that bring you to therapy, I would ask that you also focus on how you would like your circumstances to be different"). An important concluding point in goal-setting is that any agreed-to goals be as concise and concrete as possible (i.e., "How exactly might you judge that your circumstances are different enough?").

Unsuccessful Solutions

Since REFT holds that difficulties recur because of families' unsuccessful efforts to resolve them, a clear understanding of these unsuccessful efforts is critical. Emphasis is now placed on what is currently, although unsuccessfully, being done by the family members to attain their goal (resolve their complaint). A detailed description of the unsuccessful solution (A), the family belief and the rationality-irrationality which characterizes it (B), and the emotional and behavioral consequences (C) also accompanying the A and B as they are experienced during the complaint times is elicited.

Exception Times

REFT assessment next seeks to facilitate family members' examination of what happens during similar circumstances when the complaint is not occurring or has only minimal impact on their daily lives. What is occurring when the goal they have identified is being achieved in some manner? Further, what are they doing to contribute to this occurrence? Throughout this exploration, the therapist attempts to foster adherence to the basic assumption that, regardless of the magnitude or chronicity of the difficulties the family is experiencing, there are times when, for some reason, these difficulties are seemingly resolved for a period of time or only minimally influence family members' interactions, and that family members are actively contributing to the resolution. A detailed description of the successful solution (A'), the typically more rational family belief accompanying it (B') and the emotional and behavioral consequences (C') also accompanying A' and B' as they are experienced during the exception times is elicited. Consider the following family's experience.

Two parents' presenting complaint was their teenage son's noncompliance. Their goal for therapy was to have him obey them more readily. They had several specific "house rules," which if attended to more closely by the son would offer evidence that their goal had been sufficiently attained. In relaying their present efforts at attaining this goal, they reported several unsuccessful solutions: "We've warned him, taken away his allowance and other money privileges. We've grounded him for weeks at a time. We've sat him down and explained that this is our house and he has to abide by our rules. Several times, we've even hit him. We've tried to keep him away from those low-life friends of his who are constantly in trouble by sending him to private school. He was expelled after a month and a half. We've tried just about everything we can. We're totally frustrated and are beginning to be verbally abusive toward each other." The aforementioned unsuccessful solutions represent the A of this family's experience; their frustration and verbal abuse the C.

Moving on to the B, variations of the same basic irrational belief accompanied all these unsuccessful solutions: "He *must* obey us" (expressed as an absolute demand). This family belief was tied to their unsuccessful solutions and painful emotional and behavioral consequences. Assessment continued with the exploration of exception times.

Queried concerning times when circumstances were similar but the outcome different, after some reluctance the parents related several situations. One concerned a recent weekend vacation. The parents related wanting to have some "together time" as a couple and so they selected a resort where attractive activities were available for teens. They further reported deciding to let their son "take responsibility for his own enjoyment" and to not feel obligated to see that he had a good time. They described how he autonomously met some other young persons his age and had a most enjoyable weekend, only minimally interacting with the parents. The second exception time occurred only the day before the session, when both were unexpectedly called at the last minute to work at a church dinner in place of a couple who were ill. They described rushing from their home to the church and telling their son he would have to fend for himself for dinner. Upon returning home they discovered he had not only made his own dinner, but had also washed his dishes and the pans he used. Both situations were initially attributed to their belief that "he was just in a good mood." In exploring those situations further (e.g., "He may have been in a good mood, but what might the two of you have done to contribute to that good mood?"), the parents were helped to see that they had "backed off" both times. While they still expected their son to attend to the house rules, they didn't press him about doing so. They both affirmed the good feelings they had toward their son and each other during these times, as well as the pleasurable interactions that subsequently occurred among them. The aforementioned successful solutions ("backing off") represent the A' of this family's experience, their good feelings and pleasurable interactions the C'.

Moving to the B', rationally thinking that they "desired reasonable compliance" but need not demand it of their son ("We want him to attend to the house rules more closely") was tied to the more successful solutions (A') and satisfactory emotional and behavioral consequences (C').

Having now discussed assessment, we move on to the treatment intervention aspects of REFT: Debate (D) and Enactment (E).

TREATMENT: THE DE OF REFT

REFT treatment strategies revolve around facilitating family members' Debate (D) of the benefits and/or detriments of the family belief (B) that frames their unsuccessful solutions (A) and accompanying distressful emotional and behavioral consequences (C) with the family belief (B') that frames the more successful solutions (A') of the exception times and the accompanying satisfying emotional and behavioral consequences (C'). Following Debate, treatment interventions are then aimed at Enactment (E) of the rational B' in those circumstances wherein the irrational B had typically been the norm. This is all done in a manner that encourages an overall philosophy of greater rationality and constitutes the emphases of most sessions.

Debate

Webster's New Collegiate Dictionary (1976) defines "debate" as "a process wherein a question is discussed by considering opposing arguments." The Debate process of REFT is essentially equivalent to the traditional rational-emotive "Disputation" process. The term "Debate," however, has been found by the present author to promote more productive interaction among family members, given the oftentimes negative connotations attached to the term "dispute" (e.g., "quarrel") (*Webster's New Collegiate Dictionary,* 1976).

In REFT, Debate (D) is a challenge to family members to consider the opposing positions represented by their ABC (unsuccessful solutions, the irrational family belief that frames them, and the distressful feelings and behaviors they experience) and their A′ B′ C′ (more successful solutions, the rational family belief that frames them, and the more satisfying feelings and behaviors). While the ABC and A′ B′ C′ are considered in toto, the primary emphasis during Debate is on B and B′. Like traditional rational-emotive Disputation (Ellis, 1985), Debate is accomplished by engaging the family members in three important tasks (Huber & Baruth, 1989).

The first task is to facilitate considerable cognitive dissonance for family members by coupling their irrational family belief with its rational counterpart and then compiling disconfirming evidence relative to the benefits of the irrational belief. The second task involves having family members explore the rational counterpart to their irrational belief in a way that affirms the greater benefits of the rational belief. The third task is to review and confirm how the irrational belief is associated with distressful emotional and behavioral consequences, while the rational belief offers enhanced opportunity for greater emotional and behavioral satisfaction (or less dissatisfaction).

Enactment

Following successful Debate, family members are then engaged in Enactment (E). This involves rehearsing, reviewing, and confirming the step-by-step manner in which their rational B′ will characterize upcoming circumstances where their irrational B would have typically been the norm. Initially, this is accomplished through in-session interactions among family members which are monitored by the therapist. Subsequent to this, the therapist encourages family members to agree upon outside-of-session homework tasks.

As therapy progresses and family members report their circumstances as improved, the therapist reinforces the idea that the rational B′ of their former "exception time" is something they are able to get to recur through their own volition (e.g., "How did you think to make use of your more rational, successful family belief?" "What exactly were you thinking in that more successful and satisfying situation that you were not thinking when you were less satisfied?" "What are you going to think in order to experience successful solutions more regularly?"). Further, as a part of that process, the therapist also assists family members to tie emotional and behavioral consequences of greater satisfaction (or less dissatisfaction) to their efforts in enacting their rational B′ in a greater number of circumstances.

With those family members who report their circumstances as unchanged, the therapist still seeks to expand upon and enact utilization of the rational B′ of identified exception times (e.g., "It is my experience that if people don't think rationally, their situation gets worse, not just stays the same. What were you all thinking to keep things from getting worse?"). The emphasis then again moves to the rational B′ of the exception times. If family members report their circumstances as becoming worse, the therapist's emphasis would again be "What have you been thinking to prevent things from becoming *even more* troublesome than they are?" Again, the focus would be on enactment employing the rational B′ of these exception times.

These intervention strategies are pursued to the degree that ongoing therapeutic progress is evidenced. At times, family members may seem "stuck," and minimal or no meaningful progress is apparent. It is important in such circumstances that the therapist be willing to engage the family members in reassessing their original goals as well as the significance of the ABC and A′ B′ C′ earlier identified. New goals and/or a more personally significant ABC or A′ B′ C′ will typically emerge, allowing successful Debate and Enactment to take place.

EVALUATION: ASSESSING PROGRESS

REFT recognizes that there are many possible ways in which families can live normal, satisfying lives, rather than one static standard, with any deviation from that standard considered maladaptive or abnormal. Accordingly, families' presenting complaints—their statement of persistent difficulties that hinder getting on with life as they wish to pursue it, reframed as goals—are the primary focus for evaluating therapeutic progress.

Given this caveat, the most important indicator of successful REFT is a family's statement of contentment with the progress of therapy; i.e., that the goal agreed to has been sufficiently achieved and the complaint resolved. The family who enters therapy as a complainant should preferably leave as a noncomplainant. Several criteria are used, however, to qualify and quantify family members' reports.

First, as a component of assessment during the course of therapy, the therapist should regularly ask him or herself, "To what degree and with what frequency are family members: (1) utilizing the rational B' emanating from the identified exception times; and (2) moving toward an overall position of greater rationality?" Second, as family members begin to report movement from a complainant to a noncomplainant position, the therapist should inquire, "What has happened to account for the changes you see?" Again, the main evaluative criteria are reports that indicate a shift to utilizing the rational B' more frequently, as well as an overall position of increased rationality. While rational family beliefs are the obvious emphasis, it is critical that family members are actively behaving and feeling in a manner characterized by them as satisfying more consistently than they had before.

Having discussed the major components of REFT, the following case presentation illustrates their therapeutic application "in action."

CASE PRESENTATION

The client family consists of Donna, John, and a daughter, Katrice, who is 14 years old. Donna is employed as a secretary at the local university and John is a high school English teacher and coach. Katrice is in her first year of high school.

Background Information

The family reported increasing tension and overt conflict during the past several months, particularly between John and Katrice. Donna described John as having been preoccupied with his teaching and coaching responsibilities since Katrice was born. She consequently has maintained primary responsibility for Katrice's upbringing within the home. John described himself as being unable to relate adequately to Katrice when she was younger. He confirmed his preoccupation with teaching and coaching, particularly the latter, which required long hours and significant travel. He reported having recently suspended his coaching activities in order to attend classes part-time (two evenings per week) to complete his master's degree and receive a major step increase in his teaching salary.

The family reported that their present circumstances brought them together as a family more frequently. John noted that his increased presence at home has been accompanied by a desire to play a greater role in Katrice's life. He complained, however, of Katrice's lack of responsiveness toward him, as well as Donna's constant criticism of his childrearing practices, a point he finds particularly irritating given his position as a professional educator. He described himself as a "junior partner" in the marital relationship, and as being treated as "an adolescent instead of an adult." Donna reported her past requests of John to take a greater interest in Katrice and his numerous broken promises to do so. Katrice related remembrances of John continually being "too busy with his teams" to respond adequately when she had made requests of him to do things with her throughout her childhood. Both Donna and Katrice conveyed an overt desire to see John take a greater part in Katrice's life, but equally a cautious concern relative to how and whether he would actually do so.

Session Transcript

The transcript that follows is from the third session with this family. In the preceding session, assessment of the family's expectations for therapy was accomplished. After a consideration of their presenting complaints, these complaints were tied to potential therapeutic goals. The family was first engaged in brainstorming a listing of possible goals, the attainment of which would likely lead to increased resolution of their presenting complaints. From this listing, they then were assisted in prioritizing one goal they would see as having the greatest impact. Lastly, this prioritized goal was concretized by establishing "benchmarks," criteria that could be used to ascertain when their prioritized goal had been sufficiently attained. The transcript begins with a summary of the previous session's efforts in this regard.

T = *Therapist*
D = *Donna*
J = *John*
K = *Katrice*

T: Last time we got together, we identified a goal. Donna, you were saying that you saw John as having been relatively disengaged from you and Katrice for quite some time, and now he's wanting to come back in as a full family member. John, you were mentioning you saw Donna as kind of controlling and being too powerful, particularly as to how you relate with Katrice. Katrice, you agreed with your mother. In talking about that, we came up with a goal of showing greater consideration for each other's feelings; you all noted that would have a positive impact on the family. In discussing that, John, you said that you would know that your feelings were being shown greater consideration if you were consulted more often regarding Katrice and her plans by both Katrice and Donna, and maybe even on occasion had the final "yes-no" say. Donna and Katrice, you both agreed that you would see your feelings as being shown greater consideration if John, "Dad," was to be more pleasant and less authoritarian in how he addresses discipline matters with Katrice. Is that still a goal that would be compatible with what you are looking for, and that would probably have a positive impact on your family?

D: Yeah, we've been working on it.

K: I think if Dad would consider my feelings more, I would feel a lot better. That's for sure.

J: It's a good goal to shoot for.

Very early in the session, the family members are asked to recount a specific situation illustrative of their conflictual interaction; a time when they sought to realize their noted benchmarks, but were unsuccessful in doing so. As they do so, the therapist observes their individual reports, as well as their mutual interactions, and seeks to assess if the unsuccessful solution (A) in the situation they describe is a repetitive one that is representative of their complaint times. Further, the family members' emotional and behavioral experiencing in exploring this unsuccessful solution is assessed to confirm the negative consequences (C). Finally, but foremost, the therapist seeks to assess the family belief and its rationality-irrationality (B) that accompanies the A and C.

T: Donna, you noted that there have been times that you counted on John to be reasonable and relatively pleasant in how he disciplined Katrice; he wasn't, and you saw this as an example of him not showing consideration of Katrice's and your own feelings. Can you remember a time, recently, when that occurred?

D: The way he's been disciplining Katrice is, for sure, a sore point. I've always been the one to do that because John has been busy with school and everything else. I'm not that much of a disciplinarian. I run a fairly loose ship, but there's certain limits, of course. John wanting to get involved in her discipline is not what causes the problem. It's that he just gets so authoritarian when he does.

J: I just feel like if I'm not strong with her and make her do what I ask her to do, she just doesn't listen. I know she's not used to having me take a real active part, and it's just going to take a while until she gets used to it. And it just bothers me when, Donna, you interfere because it sabotages my effectiveness with Katrice, and then I have to get even harder because she just doesn't listen unless I do.

T: Was there a specific incident recently when this type of situation occurred; where, John, you were disciplining Katrice, and, Donna, you saw him as being too harsh and authoritarian? And John, you felt that you had to be more harsh and authoritarian, otherwise Katrice wouldn't listen? Can you talk about that among the three of you together, and identify one incident that you all agree occurred?

J: What about the the other day when, Katrice, you were watching TV, and Mom said "Katrice, go wash up for dinner" and you just ignored her request and kept watching TV. I was sitting in the den at my desk, and I said "Katrice, listen to your mother" and you ignored me. I then told you, "Katrice unless you turn off the TV right now, you're going to go to your room and miss your dinner."

K: Yeah, I remember that.

J: And you didn't listen, so I grabbed you by your arm and escorted you to your room screaming.

D: I just hate things like that, John. Is that necessary?

J: She would just have sat there and ignored both of us. I got her attention; I didn't hurt her or anything. I grabbed her arm firmly and escorted her to her room and closed the door and told her to stay there.

D: I feel like Katrice thinks that I'm a partner to stuff like that, and I'm not really comfortable disciplining her that way.

T: When did this situation that you're discussing occur?

K: It was last Monday evening, right?

D: Right, last Monday.

J: Yeah.

T: What were your thoughts there? What was going through your minds at that time?

J: Well, I was just thinking, "She's not listening to her mother." Her mother's not disciplining her and somebody's got to do it. I just felt really put out with Donna that she didn't get Katrice to do what she'd asked her to do. And so I just decided it's time for me to be the father and intervene. And I was angry at Donna for not being more assertive with Katrice. I was angry at Katrice for just sitting there, defiantly ignoring Donna and ignoring me. I thought, "That's enough. I'm not going to put up with that!"

T: Donna, from your perspective, how did you envision that situation? What were you thinking at that time?

D: I would have done something to get Katrice to listen to me, but I hadn't reached my limit yet. It just seemed like John interfered and did a bunch of things that didn't seem right. The whole thing got blown completely out of proportion. And it didn't seem like that was necessary.

T: So you didn't see Katrice's behavior as a problem at that time, at least not enough of a problem to address?

D: Right. It's kind of more or less what we go through as we get things done. It's the way I'm used to doing it with her.

T: Then you saw John, perhaps, as going too far and not showing consideration to your nor Katrice's feelings, given what the normal pattern has been between the two of you?

K: It seemed like he just stepped in real tough, and it's just so different from what Mom expects. I have a hard time with it. It was a major scene.

T: John, in that situation, what I heard you strongly asserting to yourself was "I *must* have my feelings considered!"

J: It felt that way. I was thinking I had to step in and get it done.

T: And so you thought you absolutely had to take over right away.

J: Yeah, I felt like I reached a limit and I just couldn't allow Katrice to behave that way any longer.

T: Donna, it sounds like you were thinking just as strongly to yourself, "If I let John take over, he goes too far. I can't give up that responsibility so easily. I *must* have my feelings considered! And Katrice's too!"

D: I feel like I'm in a bind about it, but yeah, you're right. If I do try to give up the responsibility, then it seems like he goes too far.

He doesn't consider how he hurts both Katrice and me when he does that.

T: So it sounds like your belief there was the same as John's: "I *must* have my feelings considered."

D: I guess I have really strong ideas about how you treat children and how you don't. It's easy for me to tap into some of those "how you don't" ones, for sure.

T: Katrice, it sounds like possibly you had the same thought as both your Mom and Dad in that situation: "Dad *must* consider my feelings!" You seem to have thought that particularly given what typically occurs between you and your Mom.

K: Yeah. It was like Dad was just thinking about what he was feeling and wanting there.

T: As I understand it, that was a time when all of you were really upset and felt your individual feelings were not shown enough consideration, and were demanding that you each be shown that consideration.

J: Definitely.

T: And, Donna, you said that was a time that really didn't sit well with you either. Are you still upset when you think about that?

D: I don't know about being upset, but that's the kind of stuff that pushes my buttons.

T: Katrice, it's a very unpleasant remembrance for you too?

K: Yeah, it is that.

The ABC of the family's report of a time when they were unsuccessful in realizing their noted benchmarks has been identified:

- A = Katrice not responding immediately to Donna's request, John stepping in and disciplining "harshly;"
- B = family belief of "I/We must have my/our feelings considered; and
- C = hurt and hostility among the family members.

In the dialogue that follows, the members of the family are then asked to recount a time when similar circumstances were present and when their noted benchmarks were seemingly realized, at least to some minimal degree. In observing their individual reports as well as their mutual interaction in doing so, the therapist seeks to assess if the successful solution (A′) in the situation they describe is indeed more successful than the unsuccessful A just described. Further, the family members' emotional and behavioral experiencing in exploring this successful solution is assessed to confirm the presence of more adaptive consequences (C'). Finally, but foremost, the therapist seeks to assess whether the family belief that accompanies A' and C' is clearly a rational one (B') common to all the family members.

T: That was a time that wasn't real successful for you. I assume that there have been some potentially difficult times, however, when you have *wanted* to be shown greater consideration of your feelings, but not *demanded* that this happen, and consequently felt pretty good, or at least not so bad about the situation. Can you remember a particularly tough time recently where you all were thinking that you *wanted*, but were not necessarily *demanding*, that your feelings be considered? Could I ask you to talk among yourselves for a moment, and try to think of a time? It could have been a seemingly insignificant time occurring during the course of the day.

K: Do you remember when I wanted to spend the night with my friend Karen? I asked when you were both there. Mom, you didn't say anything, but Dad, you asked, "What about the bathroom?" and said that I hadn't finished my chores.

J: I remember.

K: Dad, you didn't raise your voice, like you were mad at me for asking before my chores were finished. You said it in a nice way— like, when I finished my chores, OK.

J: I remember that. Thinking back, I thought your request was a reasonable one as long as you completed your responsibilities beforehand. You seemed to accept my request and gladly finished your chores without any complaints, which I think you often give back to me in similar situations. Without the complaining, I felt warm toward you. I mean, we had a nice evening after that. I didn't feel any hostility or the tension that we have a lot of times.

D: It just seems like those times don't happen very often. I just didn't say anything and let it go somewhat and kind of let you do things more your way. It seemed like Katrice responded much better. I don't know why.

J: She didn't argue or throw a fit or whine and say "Oh, you are being mean, you're being unfair." That's what I hear a lot.

T: Donna, you said that you felt better in that situation. You stepped back and let John take care of things, but it also sounds like you were *wanting*, but not *demanding*, that your and Katrice's feelings be given adequate consideration. What might have you been thinking there?

D: Katrice was asking for something that was kind of special. John's response to her was really a fair one. He often responds to her requests in a harsh manner and that time he was nice and matter-of-fact, as Katrice mentioned earlier. I was just thinking the situation was a fair one. If I didn't think the situation was a fair one, then I would have had a problem with it. But I didn't. It was real easy to just not be involved in it, because he was thinking about her feelings and not just his own.

T: So you were happy to see John showing consideration of Katrice's feelings, and in an indirect manner, I would assume your feelings as well, in that you desire he respond to Katrice's requests in a pleasant way?

D: Exactly.

J: Do you remember, Katrice, how you looked at Mom right after I told you what you had to do? You looked at her and she smiled. It was a supportive kind of smile—like, "Your Dad's right. You better go do that."

K: I didn't remember that right off. But I do now that you mention it.

T: John, you just described something that Donna did that sounds like you saw her as showing consideration of how you felt. You might have made the request of Katrice, but you also looked to Donna to see her response.

J: I looked over, and that's why I picked up on Katrice looking at Donna. So, yeah—Donna was there and I didn't feel like it was just my thing. I felt like I was sort of acting on behalf of both of us, on behalf of Donna and I together, and I was considering how she felt and she was considering how I felt.

T: That's a beautiful way to describe it. Donna, did you see John acting on behalf of the two of you?

D: Yeah. It wasn't him in one corner and me and/or Katrice in the other. Another way of looking at it is like we were like a team, like the way a family should be.

J: Yeah.

T: All three of you seem much more relaxed and peaceful now than when we started the session. Can you each recognize how your approaching that situation with the thought in mind, "I *want* my feelings to be considered" contributed to: 1) John, you being able to immediately respond to Katrice's request in a pleasant manner? 2) Donna, you being able to allow John and Katrice to handle that themselves, without your direct involvement? and 3) Katrice, you being able to listen to and more readily accept your Dad's response without quarrel?

J: Yeah, I do, and I'm a lot more relaxed.

K: I like it when we all agree.

D: Me too.

The A′B′C′ of the family's report of a time when they were successful in realizing their noted benchmarks has been identified:

A′ = John responding to Katrice's request in a pleasant manner and she listening and accepting his response while Donna stayed uninvolved;

B′ = family belief of "I/We want (but not demand) that my/our feelings be considered; and

C′ = more satisfaction and harmonious interactions among the family members. Debate (D) is initiated by the therapist's challenging Donna, John, and Katrice to consider the positions they have presented in describing their ABC and A′B′C′. The therapist first facilitates doubt about the rigidity of the family belief that accompanies their unsuccessful solutions and conflictual consequences. This was already accomplished initially by simply introducing an alternative perspective; that is, that there was a time recently when they *wanted* but did not necessarily *demand* consideration of their individual feelings. Debate continues through a more specific comparison of the benefits of the rational family belief that accompanied the exception time's A′ and C′ with the irrational family belief accompanying the complaint time's A and C. The objective is to affirm the greater benefits of the rational B′.

T: You just described a situation where you all were thinking to yourselves the same unspoken thought, "I *want* my feelings to be considered." Please note that I'm emphasizing the "want." You all expressed satisfaction with that situation, and the tension you frequently experience in similar situations, if there was any, either dissipated or it never even arose. This can be contrasted with the other more problematic situation that you described earlier, where you were all thinking another unspoken thought: "I *must* have my feelings considered!" Here note that I'm stressing the "must." Then there was a lot of emotional tension and awkward, negative actions. Consequently, what I would ask you is, if you had a choice, and relating back to your goal for therapy, which is a more beneficial belief for you: "I *want* my feelings considered" or "I *must* have my feelings considered"?

J: Well, I'll tell you, everytime we get into the "must" thing, into that demanding kind of stuff, it causes problems.

D: Yeah, that's an interesting way of looking at it. I didn't exactly think, "Well, I want my feelings to be considered," but I did experience it like that even without consciously thinking it.

K: We were different after that too. I mean, we were different together after that.

J: Yeah. It was nice. It really was.

Following successful Debate, the therapist then moves to Enactment (E) to facilitate the family's rehearsing, reviewing, and confirming the step-by-step manner in which their rational family belief might be applied more frequently. John, Donna, and Katrice are assisted in interacting in the session relative to how they might employ the session understandings in the coming week among themselves. Enactment further offers an opportunity to confirm the family's willingness and ability to employ a position of greater rationality inherent in the rational family belief they have acknowledged to be more beneficial.

T: Donna, you describe your belief about the situation in a very poetic sort of way, how you "experienced it." You used the term "interesting" and I would ask you, given that interest, if we might now attempt to anticipate a scenario that will be arising during the coming week. Is there any potentially tension-filled situation that's likely to occur among the three of you?

D: Well, the recurring one is the one that we're having so much trouble with—just getting the three of us together at dinner time.

T: John and Katrice, do you also see that as a situation in which you anticipate experiencing some tension among yourselves and Donna—Mom?

J: The thing with Katrice not paying attention and dawdling and not coming to dinner—the same thing happens in the mornings with getting her up and getting her off to school. She doesn't listen and I end up having to yell at her to do these things and it's not pleasant.

T: Listen to what you said just now: "I have to yell at her to do these things." It sounds like you're going back to that thought of "I *must* have the way I feel considered and adhered to absolutely!"

J: Yeah—that is a real strong belief for me, I guess. I mean, this is a pattern that we've had for a long time.

T: Let me back you up. How about dinner time? It sounds like a potentially tension-filled time that you all see as similarly problematic. Could I ask the three of you to put the belief "I want my feelings to be considered" firmly in your minds? Again, I would stress the "want" as opposed to "must." Now, can you talk about how you might actually do that relative to dinnertime? How about if—not tonight . . . I don't know how your dinner situation is going to be tonight—but maybe tomorrow. Would you talk about that with each other with that thought firmly in mind? "I want to, not *must,* have my feelings considered."

K: You know, Dad, I think I'm finally hearing you say that my dawdling was driving you crazy. Perhaps if we decided ahead of time— you could just tell me when dinner was ready and you would call me and not wait for Mom to do so? I think I'd be able to come more quickly, knowing how important it is for you.

J: You'd get a clear message. You'd feel OK about me doing that?

K: I think as long as it was just clear what was expected. Mom never minds giving me several calls before I have to actually come to the table.

J: Donna, I think it could work if you would communicate to Katrice and me that you wouldn't see your feelings as being ignored— that it's your wish too that I do this.

D: You're probably right. I mean it's probably just she and I playing on one side against you on the other.

T: So you are looking to be more considerate of each other's feelings as well as wanting your own to be better acknowledged, then . . . is that what you're saying?

D: Yeah. I do feel that way.

T: And John and Katrice?

J: Yeah. Sure. I think it would be great. I'd like to try it.

K: Me too.

T: When do you think you can start out with that?

J: Well, we are going out to eat tonight. Tomorrow night I guess.

John, Donna, and Katrice continued in therapy for 3 more sessions following the session transcribed here for a total of six sessions. During the sixth session, it was mutually determined that they had sufficiently achieved their stated goal, their benchmarks were sufficiently realized, and their presenting complaint was sufficiently resolved. The criteria used to qualify and quantify family members' reports included:

1.   they were increasingly utilizing the rational B′ ("wanting") emanating from their identified exception times during in-session enactments;

2.   when asked, "What has been occurring to account for the changes you see?" they attributed the changes they experienced to utilizing the rational B′ in their mutual interactions more frequently and in a consciously planned manner; and

3.   all reported actively behaving and feeling in a manner characterized by them as more satisfying and harmonious.

DISCUSSION

Every psychotherapeutic approach, either explicitly or implicitly, suggests how it should be viewed in the context of other viewpoints. REFT is conceived of and offered in this chapter as a "clinical perspective." As an essentially clinical rather than an academic or research perspective, REFT represents an evolving set of practical, clinical procedures providing several distinct advantages (Huber & Baruth, 1989).

Family systems do not necessarily behave on the basis of observable words, actions, and emotions alone, but always on the basis of these observable forms of human expression *and* the covert beliefs of family members about their own and others' behaviors. REFT is concerned especially with making the contribution of family members' beliefs very plain. It posits particularly how certain types of beliefs are crucial accompaniments to the existence and persistence of recurring difficulties as well as to their alleviation. Here it is noted that *family beliefs are not necessarily the same as the individual beliefs of each of the family members; they are a "common" belief that influences the manner in which family members interact.*

This latter point was highlighted in the case presentation. John, Donna, and Katrice were each individually thinking, respectively: "Donna should be more firm in her disciplining of Katrice"; "John should be less authoritarian in his disciplining of Katrice"; and "Dad's only thinking about himself." "Traditional" Rational Emotive Behavior Therapy would propose that these individual beliefs be accorded primacy in treatment (DiGiuseppe & Zeeve, 1985). REFT, by contrast, accords primacy to the treatment of the family's commonly held family belief. In the case presented here, the belief was "My individual feelings *must* be considered." From a clinical perspective, the opportunity for simplifying the treatment process by reducing the number of variables (i.e., beliefs) under consideration is clear (Huber & Backlund, 1991). Greater efficiency and effectiveness in the immediacy of the treatment milieu and long-term recall of critical cognitions consequently occur.

While REFT pragmatically presupposes the primacy of family beliefs in treatment, it does not presuppose these beliefs to be the only focus; effective family therapy involves considering and dealing with a number of interrelated factors. REFT's ABC, A'B'C', and DE alert the therapist and client family to the importance of certain specific process elements, thereby escaping the often bewildering array of extraneous content issues that are available for consideration. Not only are the B and B' elements important, but so is assessing the A, C, A', and C' and then actively engaging in D and E. All are critical. All simultaneously occur within the interactions that constitute family functioning from a family systems perspective.

The case presentation used in this chapter particularly highlighted REFT's identification of the rational B' as well as investigating the accompanying A' and C' of the exception times. The therapist worked from the REFT assumption that the family had areas of competence upon which to draw in order to surmount their expressed concerns. It was assumed that there were "exception times" when John, Donna, and Katrice mutually interacted in a manner characterized by a more rational family belief. This belief, their successful solutions, and accompanying satisfying emotional and behavioral consequences had simply been discounted in concert with the family's absolutist irrational family belief, their recurrent unsuccessful solutions, and accompanying distressful emotional and behavioral consequences. Herein too, from a clinical perspective, the opportunity for simplifying the process by utilizing skills and understandings already in the family's repertoire is clear (Huber & Driskill, 1993). Again, greater efficiency and effectiveness in the immediacy of the treatment milieu and more ready identification of critical cognitions consequently occur.

REFERENCES

de Shazer, S., Berg, J. K., Lipchik, E., Nunnally, E., Molnar, A., Gingerich, W., & Weiner-Davis, M. (1986). Brief therapy: Focused solution development. *Family Process, 25,* 207–221.

DiGiuseppe, R., & Zeeve, C. (1985). Marriage: Rational-emotive couples counseling. In A. Ellis & M. Bernard (Eds.), *Clinical applications of rational-emotive therapy* (pp. 55–80). New York: Plenum.

Dryden, W. (1984). *Rational-emotive therapy: Fundamentals and innovations.* London: Croom Helm.

Ellis, A. (1985). What is rational-emotive therapy? In A. Ellis & M. Bernard (Eds.), *Clinical applications of rational-emotive therapy* (pp. 1–30). New York: Plenum.

Ellis, A. (1987). The impossibility of achieving consistently good mental health. *American Psychologist, 42,* 364–375.

Ellis, A. (1993). Fundamentals of rational-emotive therapy for the 1990's. In W. Dryden & L. K. Hill (Eds.), *Innovations in rational-emotive therapy* (pp. 1–32). Newbury Park, CA: Sage.

Fisch, R., Weakland, J., & Segal, L. (1982). *The tactics of change: Doing therapy briefly.* San Francisco: Jossey-Bass.

Huber, C. H., & Backlund, B. A. (1991). *The twenty minute counselor: Transforming brief conversations into effective helping experiences.* New York: Continuum.

Huber, C. H., & Baruth, L. G. (1989). *Rational-emotive family therapy: A systems perspective.* New York: Springer.

Huber, C. H., & Driskill, P. G. (1993). *Equilibrium family therapy: A basic guide for the helping professions.* New York: Crossroad.

Jackson, D. (1977). The study of the family. In P. Watzlawick & J. Weakland (Eds.), *The interactional view* (pp. 2–21). New York: Norton.

O'Hanlon, W. H., & Weiner-Davis, M. (1989). *In search of solutions.* New York: Norton.

Webster's new collegiate dictionary (1976). Springfield, MA: G. & C. Merriam.

Wessler, R. A., & Wessler, R. L. (1980). *The principles and practice of rational-emotive therapy.* San Francisco: Jossey-Bass.

CHAPTER 6

REBT and Its Application to Group Therapy

Albert Ellis

I began to do group therapy in 1949 with adolescents at the New Jersey State Diagnostic Center when I was still practicing psychoanalysis, and got reasonably good results helping my delinquent clients to open up and reveal themselves. I helped them to accept responsibility for their delinquencies, to work with other group members, to understand themselves, and to make some useful changes. But I soon discovered that psychoanalytic group therapy, like psychoanalytic individual psychotherapy, was woefully inefficient for several reasons:

1. It focused on people's past, especially their early life, mistakenly assuming that *that* made them disturbed.
2. It gave them false explanations for their neurosis (and other personality problems), especially the idea that unfortunate or traumatic Activating Experiences (A's) gave them neurotic Consequences (C's), no matter what they Believed (B) about these A's.
3. It obsessively explored their "transference" relationships with their therapists and other group members and assumed that these were caused by prior deep relationships in their childhood.

131

4. It deified the expression of group members' feelings and wrongly held that if they got in full touch with these feelings and honestly expressed them they would win the approval of others and minimize their serious phobias of panic, depression, and rage (Ellis, 1962, 1968; Ellis & Harper, 1961, 1975; Yalom, 1985).

For the first several years that I was in full-time practice in New York City, and even when I started doing REBT with my individual clients in 1955, I still avoided doing group therapy because of its usual insufficiencies. But I saw that one analyst had three of my individual clients in his groups, and that almost every time they attended his group sessions they became more disturbed, while after most of their individual sessions with me they became less disturbed. So I decided, in 1959, to start my first REBT group; soon had 5 of these groups going—and going strong—every week, and discovered that for most clients most of the time, my kind of group therapy was more effective, often in a brief period, than was my individual therapy—and much more effective than any form of psychoanalysis. Why? For several reasons:

1. In individual therapy, I mainly Dispute and show my clients how to Dispute their self-defeating irrational Beliefs (iBs). But in group therapy, several other group members do active Disputing and thereby present better and stronger Disputation.

2. In individual therapy, clients rarely get practice in talking me out of my iBs (because we are mainly focusing on them and their iBs). But in group they have many opportunities to discover others' iBs, to actively Dispute them, and thereby receive excellent practice in Disputing their own similar irrationalities.

3. In group therapy, all the group members can, and often do, suggest bigger and better homework assignments for each of the other members.

4. When accepting homework, group members are more likely to carry it out than individual therapy clients, because they have to report back to the whole group as to whether or not they actually did it.

5. When people feel very upset during group sessions, which they often do, we can immediately zero in on what they are telling themselves to help them, right in the here and now, to undo their upsetness and to work to give it up.

6.   Homework assignments and other emotive-evocative exercises, which are often used in Rational Emotive Behavior Therapy, can be carried out during group sessions, and not just outside of therapy. Thus, my groups are often given—or give themselves—shame-attacking, secret-revealing, hot-seat, risk-taking, and other encounter-type exercises in the course of regular group sessions and are then able to express their feelings about these exercises and to receive feedback from the therapist and from other group members.

7.   The many cognitive, emotive and behavioral methods that are commonly used in individual REBT can also be employed in group REBT—and, again, feedback from and interactions with other group members often adds to these methods' effectiveness.

8.   Most people come to REBT (and other forms of therapy) with some significant interpersonal and relationship problems. Because the group is a *social* situation, many such problems may be more easily assessed and worked on than they often can be in individual treatment (Ellis, 1982, 1990).

KINDS OF REBT GROUPS

Most of my groups are small, weekly-held groups, lasting two and a quarter hours. They include a maximum of 10 people, because REBT small group sessions are less rambling and more structured than other kinds of groups, and can include more than the six or eight members that other therapies usually set as their top limits. My own groups include males and females, usually ranging from 18 to 70 years of age, with many different kinds of problems and disturbances.

However, at the psychological clinic of the Institute for Rational-Emotive Therapy in New York, we also have some same-sex groups, for men and women who prefer to open up only in such a group. We also have time-limited groups—usually for only six or eight sessions—where all the members have a main common problem such as neurotic procrastination, overeating, relationship troubles, anxiety, or hostility. In addition, we regularly arrange 1- to 2-day rational encounter marathons and 9-hour large group intensives (with 50 or more people at a time).

We also have my famous Friday night workshop, "Problems of Daily Living," with as many as 150 people in the audience watching while I (or if I am out of town, one of my main associates, such as Dr. Janet L. Wolfe or Dr. Dominic DiMattia) interview individual volunteer clients in public and then throw the discussion of the interview open to all the members of the audience who choose to participate (Dryden, Backx, & Ellis, 1987; Ellis, Sichel, Leaf, & Mass, 1989).

Again, we have regular 4-hour workshops, with from 10 to 90 participants, in special topics such as managing difficult people, creative personal encounters, panic disorders, post-traumatic stress disorders, and sexual problems (Institute for Rational-Emotive Therapy, 1994).

SELECTING PARTICIPANTS FOR ONGOING GROUPS

No one is usually allowed into any of my ongoing small groups at the Institute for Rational-Emotive Therapy in New York City unless he or she has had at least one individual therapy session. Often, potential members have a number of individual sessions at the Institute before joining group; and only if their individual therapist thinks that they are unsuitable for the group process are they refused entry into a group.

If people desire to become group members without having previous individual sessions, they are required to have at least one individual interview for screening purposes. They are almost always allowed to enter a group, even if they are seriously neurotic, have a personality disorder, or have some psychotic behaviors, as long as they are not considered to be disruptive and too combative. Thus, those who are compulsive talkers, who have frequent angry outbursts at other group members, who are too narcissistic, who come to group under the influence of alcohol or other substances, who cannot follow normal group procedures, or who otherwise would take up too much time in group or would prove unhelpful to other members are not admitted. If they somehow do get into one of my groups, they are dealt with very firmly and trained to be more "normal" group participants. Or else they are told to enter individual therapy and only to return when their individual therapist advises that they are ready to do so.

A few members are also dropped from group when they violate its basic rules, such as that they remain confidential outside of group about everything that goes on during the group sessions. In conducting my regular groups steadily since 1959, and having many hundreds of different participants, I (in collaboration with other members of the group) have only insisted that less than 10 people leave the group. However, several dozen more have participated so poorly in group that they have spontaneously seen that they are not suitable members and have quit on their own. Frequently, instead, they have gone into individual therapy with myself or other therapists at the Institute.

PROCEDURE OF SMALL GROUP REGULAR SESSIONS

REBT small group sessions can be arranged with different procedures and still be effective. I run my own five weekly groups at the Institute as follows. I usually start each session by asking each member, one at a time, whether she or he has done the agreed-upon last homework assignment (a list of which I have in front of me). "If not," I ask, "Why not?" I look for the dysfunctional, irrational Beliefs (iBs) that probably stopped her or him from doing the homework, such as: "It's *too* hard to do it. I *should* improve without doing it!" Or: "I *have* to show myself and the group that I'll do it beautifully. Else, I'm a no-goodnik!" I and other group members Dispute this person's low frustration tolerance (LFT) and perfectionism, and encourage her or him to do the assignment next week and/or modify it or add to it.

We then ask the member what disturbances occurred this week, what irrational Beliefs (iBs) accompanied these disturbances, what was done to Dispute them, what other REBT techniques were used, what progress or lack of progress was made, what could best be done now, etc. If the group is working well, I alone don't merely question, challenge, and encourage each member, but several other members also do so, and there is much lively interaction and interchange.

By the time each session ends, all the members present have usually been checked on their homework, led to discuss continuing or new problems, shown how their iBs are often remarkably similar to other members' dysfunctional Beliefs, led to do some active Disputing, helped to discuss other REBT methods they can use, encouraged to talk to other members and to help them, and asked to accept another homework assignment.

If time runs out before important issues can be discussed, they are put on the agenda for priority handling during the following session (Ellis, 1992).

USEFUL REBT GROUP TECHNIQUES

As noted previously, nearly all the regular REBT techniques are sometimes used during group therapy sessions, as well as some encounter-type exercises that are specially designed for group processes. Here are some of the techniques that have been found to be most useful.

Cognitive Techniques of REBT

Active disputing. Members are all taught the ABCs of REBT, shown how to find their self-defeating, absolutist shoulds and musts, their awfulizing, their I-can't-stand-it-itis, their damning of self and of other persons, their overgeneralizations, and their other dysfunctional inferences and attributions and are shown how to Dispute these with empirical, logical, and pragmatically useful challenges. As noted above, they are given much practice in Disputing others' irrationalities as well as their own (Bernard, 1991, 1993; Dryden, 1994; Dryden & DiGiuseppe, 1990; Ellis, 1962, 1973, 1985, 1988; Ellis & Dryden, 1996; Ellis & Grieger, 1977, 1986; Ellis & Harper, 1975; Walen, DiGiuseppe, & Dryden, 1992; Yankura & Dryden, 1990).

Rational coping self-statements. In group and in their outside life, members are encouraged to prepare rational Beliefs (rBs) and coping statements to substitute for their iBs, and to keep using them steadily until they consistently believe and act on them. Such self-statements can be factual and encouraging (e.g., "I am able to succeed on this job, and I'll work hard to show that I can"). Or, preferably, they can be more philosophical (e.g., "I'd like very much to succeed but I don't *have to* do so; and if I fail I am never a failure or a worthless individual") (Dryden, 1994; Ellis, 1957, 1988; Yankura & Dryden, 1990).

Referenting. Group members can make a list of the real disadvantages of their harmful addictions (e.g., smoking) and a list of the real advantages of changing their dysfunctional behaviors (e.g., procrastination or avoidance of sex-love relationships). They can review and think about this list several times every day (Danysh, 1974; Ellis & Velten, 1992).

Modeling. Participants are urged to model themselves after the healthy behavior of the leader, of another member, of friends or relatives, or of other good models they hear of or read about (Bandura, 1986; Ellis & Abrams, 1994).

Cognitive homework. Members use the ABCDEs of REBT, observe some of their unfortunate Adversities (A's), figure out their iBs, Dispute them (at D) and arrive at Effective New Philosophies (E). They do so, either in their head or on one of the RET Self-Help Forms (Sichel & Ellis, 1984).

Psychoeducational techniques. Group members use REBT books, workbooks, pamphlets, audio-video cassettes, and other self-help materials to understand and solidify their working at REBT cognitive, emotive, and behavioral methods (Ellis & Abrams, 1994; Ellis & Lange, 1994; Ellis & Velten, 1992).

Proselytizing. Members are encouraged to use REBT to try to help other members, as well as their friends and relatives, to overcome their iBs and thereby help themselves overcome their own disturbances (Ellis & Abrahms, 1978).

Recording therapy sessions. Participants may record the parts of their sessions where the other participants are largely trying to help them with their personal problems, and listen to these recordings in between the sessions (Ellis & Abrahms, 1978; Ellis & Velten, 1992).

Reframing. Members are shown how to look for unfortunate A's to see that they include good things as well. They learn to accept the challenge, when "bad" A's occur, of making themselves healthfully sorry and frustrated, rather than unhealthily panicked and depressed (Ellis, 1985, 1988).

Emotive Techniques of REBT

Forceful coping self-statements. REBT hypothesizes that group members (and other people) often hold their iBs quite strongly (with "hot" cognitions) and that, therefore, they had better vigorously and powerfully think, feel, and act against them (Ellis, 1969b; Ellis & Abrahms, 1978; Ellis & Harper, 1975). Among its emotive-evocative methods is the use of forceful coping self-statements—such as, "I NEVER, NEVER need what I want. I ONLY prefer it!" "I can ALWAYS accept *myself*, my personhood, even when I do stupid and wrong *acts!*" (Bernard & Wolfe, 1993; Ellis, 1985, 1988; Ellis & Abrahms, 1978; Ellis & Velten, 1992).

Rational Emotive Imagery. Maxie Maultsby, Jr., an REBT psychiatrist, created rational emotive imagery (REI) in 1971, and I added more emotive and behavioral elements to it (Ellis, 1993; Maultsby, 1971; Maultsby & Ellis, 1974). Group members do REI, both during group sessions and as homework, by imagining one of the worst things that could happen to them (e.g., continuing failure); letting themselves feel very upset about this image (e.g., panicked); imploding this disturbed feeling; and then working on their feeling, to make themselves have healthy or appropriate negative feelings (such as sorrow, disappointment, or frustration). They can do this every day for 30 days (it usually takes only a minute or two to do so) until they automatically experience their healthy negative feelings when they imagine, or actually encounter, similar "horrible" happenings.

Role-playing. Group members often role-play with other group members or with the therapist, as when they play the interviewee for an important job and the other plays the interviewer. During this form of behavior rehearsal, the rest of the group critiques how well the member is doing in the role-play and suggests how she or he could improve. If either of the role-players shows anxiety, the role-play is temporarily stopped and this person is asked what he or she was thinking to create the anxiety and how he or she could think, instead, to allay it (Corsini, 1957; Ellis & Abrahms, 1978; Moreno, 1990).

Reverse role-play. One group member takes another's irrational Belief (e.g., "So-and-so must always love me completely!") and holds on to it rigidly and forcefully while playing the irrational member's role. The person with the iB then has to talk the other roleplayer—actually himself or herself—out of this firmly held iB (Ellis & Abrams, 1994; Ellis, Abrams, & Dengelegi, 1992).

Forceful taped disputing. A group member tapes one of his or her main iBs as homework (e.g., "Everybody always has to treat me fairly!") and vigorously Disputes it on the same tape. The other members listen to the Disputing to see if it is really rational and also to see how vigorous and forceful it is (Ellis, 1985, 1988).

Use of humor. Members are shown how to not take themselves and their mistakes too seriously, and encouraged to humorously assail the iBs of other group members—but only to put down and laugh at the other's ideas and behaviors, and not to denigrate the person himself or herself (Ellis, 1977a, 1977b). REBT group members at the psychological clinic of the Institute for Rational-Emotive Therapy in New York City are given a group of rational humorous songs to sing to themselves when they feel panicked, depressed, or enraged. The whole group, as an exercise, may also sing some of these humorous songs or others which they create or contribute to the group themselves. A typical rational humorous song is:

I WISH I WERE NOT CRAZY![1]

(Tune: *Dixie,* by Dan Emmett)

Oh, I wish I were really put together—
Smooth and fine as patent leather!
Oh, how great to be rated innately sedate!
But I'm afraid that I was fated
To be rather aberrated—

Oh, how sad to be mad as my Mom and my Dad!
Oh, I wish I were not crazy! Hooray, hooray!
I wish my mind were less inclined
To be the kind that's hazy!
I could agree to really be less crazy.
But I, alas, am just too goddamned lazy!

---

[1] Lyrics by Albert Ellis, Copyright 1977 by the Institute for Rational-Emotive Therapy.

Relationship methods. Members are given unconditional self-acceptance (USA) by the therapist, no matter how badly or selfishly they behave, and are taught how to give it to other group members and to people outside the group. They are helped to relate better to people in their regular lives and are often taught interpersonal and social skills training in the group (Dryden, 1994; Ellis, 1957, 1973; Ellis & Harper, 1975; Franklin, 1993; Hauck, 1992; Mills, 1993).

Encouragement. Members are encouraged to encourage other troubled members to think, feel, and act less disturbedly and more enjoyably, and to do their therapeutic homework, even when it is arduous or difficult to do (Ansbacher & Ansbacher, 1956; Ellis, 1957, 1991; Losoncy, 1980).

Encounter exercises. Members are given group encounter exercises in their regular group and in special all-day marathons that are arranged for them once or twice a year. Nine-hour intensives are also run by the Institute for Rational-Emotive Therapy in New York for group members (and other people) who want to participate in larger-scale group exercises (Ellis, 1969b, 1992; Ellis, Sichel, Leaf, & Mass, 1989).

Behavioral Techniques of REBT

In vivo desensitization. Group members are encouraged to do a number of harmless acts, such as making a public speech or talking to strangers, that they are neurotically afraid to do, and also to use several other active-experiential behavioral methods of REBT. They are encouraged to use exposure to past or present traumatic scenes in order to face and work through their horror of imagining or thinking about traumas in their lives, particularly if they have post-traumatic stress disorder (PTSD) or other forms of panic (Bernard, 1991, 1993; Dryden, 1994; Ellis, 1962, 1994; Ellis & Abrams, 1994; Ellis & Velten, 1992; Moore, 1993; Walen, DiGiuseppe & Dryden, 1992).

Avoiding running away from obnoxious events. When group members find other members obnoxious or "horrible" and overreact to them they are encouraged *not* to leave the group until they modify their feelings of rage or horror—and to practice doing so in spite of the "terrible" situation they are in. Once they make themselves considerably less disturbed, they are advised to *then* decide whether it is more advantageous or disadvantageous for them to tolerate being with "obnoxious" group members. Similarly, they are often encouraged not to run away from "bad" people outside the group until they modify their rage or I-can't-stand-it-itis about staying with these people (Ellis & Abrahms, 1978).

Use of reinforcement. Being strongly behavioral, REBT shows group members how to suitably reinforce themselves by doing something enjoyable only after they have done something onerous—such as working on a term paper—that they are neurotically avoiding. In group itself they may be allowed to speak up about their own problems only *after* they have tried to help other members with their difficulties (Ellis, 1969a, 1982, 1990).

Use of penalties. Many clients won't stop their addictive or compulsive behavior because it is too immediately pleasurable or reinforcing; and they will not change it for a normal reinforcement. Thus, they will not give up smoking or problem drinking for allowing themselves to read or enjoy television. Consequently, REBT encourages some group members to severely penalize themselves after their destructive indulgences—for example, to spend an hour with a boring person every time they gamble, or light every cigarette they smoke with a $20 bill. Clients also encourage other group members to enact suitable penalties and monitor their doing so (Dryden, 1994; Ellis & Abrams, 1994; Ellis, Abrams & Dengelegi, 1992; Ellis & Velten, 1992).

Skill training. Group members often learn and practice particular important interpersonal skills in the group sessions, for example, learning to listen to others, accepting them with their poor behavior, communicating openly with them, and forming relationships with them. They are also urged to acquire suitable personal and interpersonal skills by taking courses and practicing outside of group (Ellis, 1976, 1977c).

Relapse prevention. Members are shown how to ward off relapses, to accept themselves when they relapse, and to revert to self-helping thoughts, feelings, and behaviors when they fall back to disturbed behavior. To do this, they are taught the relapse prevention methods of Marlatt and Gordon (1989) and other cognitive behaviorists and the specific relapse-preventive methods of REBT—particularly monitoring and Disputing their own musturbatory[2] philosophies that lead to relapse (Ellis, McInerney, DiGiuseppe, & Yeager, 1988; Ellis, 1992; Ellis & Velten, 1992).

PROCESSES OF REBT GROUP THERAPY

Various theorists and practitioners have described processes that therapy groups and their leaders go through, or are supposed to go through (Bennett, 1984; Lazarus, 1968; Rogers, 1980; Rose, 1980; Upper & Rose, 1980; Yalom, 1985). Some of these processes are emphasized in REBT groups and some are not. Let me discuss them in the light of my previous discussion (Ellis, 1992) which I shall now revise and bring up to date.

Transference

REBT views transference, first, as overgeneralization. Thus, because group members were once treated badly by their fathers and treated well by their mothers, they may tend to put other males in the same category as their father, and may feel hostile or indifferent to men and warm toward women. They may—or may not!—also react to the therapist as a father/mother figure and to other group members as siblings. These are overgeneralizations but, unless they are extreme, may not lead to major emotional and behavioral problems. Because REBT is not preoccupied with this kind of transference (as psychoanalysis is), it does not obsessively look for it and consequently invariably "find" it.

When normal, nondisturbed transference reactions are observed in my groups, I largely ignore them; but when they escalate into disturbed reactions in the group itself or in the members' personal lives, the other group members and I point to these reactions and show mem-

---

[2] Editors' note: The term *musturbatory* was coined by Ellis to describe an individual's beliefs when they are rigid, demanding, and absolutistic in nature. Thus, Ellis occasionally makes reference to clients' "musturbatory beliefs" or "musturbatory philosophies."

bers how destructive they are and how to minimize them. Thus, if Miriam avoids sex-love relationships because her father kept rejecting her, we show her that all males are *not* her father, that she can sensibly choose a different type of man, and that if she makes a mistake and picks a partner who is as unloving as her father, that doesn't prove that she needs his love, that she is worthless without it, nor that she'll never be able to have a long-term loving relationship. The group and I dispute her disturbed overgeneralizing but not her normal generalizing.

Similarly, if a male member deifies or devil-ifies me, the group leader, and sees me as a loved or hated father figure, we point out his disturbed transference reactions, show him the distorted thinking that lies behind it, and encourage him to adopt less dysfunctional thoughts, feelings, and behaviors. Or if a woman fights with female group members just as she fights with her sisters, we point out her transference and the irrational cognitions behind it and show her how to break her rigid women-are-all-like-my-sisters reaction.

The term *transference* is also used in psychotherapy to denote the close relationship that usually develops between clients and their therapist. I find that such relationship factors do develop in my group, but not nearly as intensely as they do with my individual therapy clients. However, REBT actively espouses the therapist's giving all clients close attention, showing real interest in helping them solve their problems, and—especially—giving what Rogers (1961) calls unconditional positive regard and what I (Ellis, 1973, 1985, 1988; Ellis & Harper, 1975) have called *unconditional acceptance*. So, although I am often confrontational with group members, I try to show them that I really care about helping them; that I will work hard to hear, understand, and empathize with them; that I have great faith that they can, despite their handicaps, improve; that I can poke fun *at their irrationalities* without laughing *at them;* and that I totally accept them as fallible humans, no matter how badly they often think and behave. I also use my *person* in my group sessions, and consequently am informal, take risks, reveal some of my own feelings, tell jokes and stories, and generally am myself as well as a group leader. In this way, I hope to model flexible, involved, nondisturbed behaviors.

Countertransference

I frankly like and dislike some of my group members more than I do others, and I especially tend to dislike members who often come late, act unhelpfully to others, fail to do their homework, and behave disruptively in group. When I see that I am feeling this way, I look for my possibly telling myself, "They *shouldn't* be the way they are and are rotten shits for being that way!" I immediately dispute those damning beliefs and convince myself, "They *should* act the poor way that they do, because it is their nature to act that way right now. I dislike what they do but I can accept *them* with their unfortunate *doings.*"

By decreasing my *demands* on my clients, I largely (not completely) overcome my negative countertransference, and I am able to deal with "bad" group members more therapeutically. I sometimes, depending on their vulnerability, confront them and honestly tell them, "I try not to hate *you*, but I really do dislike some of your *behavior*, and I hope for my sake, the group's sake, and especially your own sake, that you change it." When I find myself prejudicedly favoring some members of my groups, I convince myself that they are not gods or goddesses, and I make an effort to keep liking them personally without unduly favoring them in group.

Methods of Intervention

Most of my interventions take place with each individual member as he is telling about his homework, talking about his progress and lack of progress, presenting new problems, or returning to old ones. I speak directly to him, ask questions, make suggestions, ferret out and dispute his dysfunctional thoughts, feelings, and behaviors, and suggest homework. My interventions are mainly about his personal problems, especially as they relate to his outside life, but also as they relate to what he says and doesn't say in group.

I often show a member that her actions (and inactions) in group may well replicate her out-of-group behaviors. Thus, I may say, "Johanna, you speak so low here that we can hardly hear what you say. Do you act the same way in social groups? If so, what are you telling yourself to *make* yourself speak so low?"

My interpersonal interventions include commenting on how group members react to each other; noting that they often fail to speak up to or interact with other members; noting their warm or hostile reactions to others, and encouraging the former and questioning the latter; giving them relationship exercises to do during group sessions; having a personal interaction with some of the members; and, especially, pointing out that their group interactions may indicate how they sabotage themselves in their outside relationships and giving them some in-group skill training that may help them relate better outside the group.

My intervention with the group as a whole largely consists of giving all its members cognitive, emotive, and behavioral exercises to be done in the group; giving them all the same homework exercise, such as a shame-attacking exercise, to do before the next session; giving them a brief lecture on one of the main theories or practices of REBT; and explaining to them some of the group procedures and discussing with them the advantages and disadvantages of these procedures.

Most of the time, as noted above, I intervene on the individual level, but when interpersonal problems—such as two or more members failing to relate to each other—arise, I often intervene with duos or trios. I also plan in advance group-as-a-whole interventions, or else I spontaneously promote them as I deem them advisable (or as the spirit moves me!).

Focusing on Group Processes

Most of the time in my group sessions I use an individualized content focus. I assume that the group members come to therapy to work on their own individual problems and mainly to help themselves in their outside lives. Therefore, I induce them largely to talk about the things that are bothering them in their self-oriented and interpersonal relationships and, with the help of the group, try to show them how they are needlessly upsetting themselves in their daily lives and what they can do to think, feel, and act more healthfully.

The purpose of REBT group (and individual) therapy is to show clients how they are not only assessing and blaming *what they do* but also damning *themselves* for doing it; how they are also evaluating others' behavior *and* damning these others for their "bad" behavior; and how they are noting environmental difficulties and (externally and internally) whining about them, instead of constructively trying to change or avoid them. Therefore, whenever members bring up any undue or exaggerated upsetness, and feel unhealthily panicked, depressed, self-hating, and enraged (instead of healthily sad, disappointed, and frustrated) when unfortunate events occur, the other members and I focus on showing them what they are doing to upset themselves needlessly, how to stop doing this, and how to plan and act on achieving a more fulfilling, happier existence. When they are, as it were, "on stage" in the group, almost everyone focuses on them and their difficulties and tries to help them overcome these in the group itself and in the outside world. So a majority of the time in each session is spent on dealing with individual members' problems.

When, however, any of the members displays a problem that particularly relates to the group itself, this is dealt with specifically and group-wise. Thus, if a member keeps coming quite late to group or is absent a good deal of the time, either I or other members raise this as an issue, and we speak to this member about it. We determine, for instance, why he comes late, what core philosophies encourage him to do so, how he defeats himself and the other members by his lateness, how he can change, and what kind of homework assignment in this respect he will agree to carry out. At the same time, the general problem of lateness—as it relates to group and also as it relates to the members' outside lives—is also frequently discussed, and it is brought out how latecoming is disadvantageous to other members and how it interferes with a cohesive and beneficial group process.

Similarly, if a group member only speaks about her own problems and doesn't take the risk of speaking to the others, disputing their self-defeating thoughts and behaviors, and making some suitable suggestions for their change, she is questioned about this and shown how and why she is blocking herself in group, and how and why she probably behaves similarly in her outside life. But the general problem of members being too reserved—or, sometimes, too talkative—in group is also raised, and various members are encouraged to speak up about this problem and to give their ideas about how the group process would be more effective if virtually all the members talked up appropriately, rather than said too much or too little.

Also, if the group as a whole seems to be functioning poorly—for example, being dull, uninterested, apathetic, or overly boisterous—I raise this issue, encourage a general discussion of it, get members to suggest alternative ways for the group to act, and check on these suggestions later to see if they are being implemented. Once in a while I go over some of the general principles of REBT—such as the theory that people largely upset themselves rather than *get* upset—to make sure that the members as a whole understand these principles and are better prepared to use them during the sessions and in their outside affairs.

I keep looking for cues for underlying issues that are not being handled well in group. Some cues are members only being interested in their own problems and not those of other members; not being alert during the group; being too negative to other members who may not be working at helping themselves improve; giving only practical advice to other members, rather than disputing their irrational philosophies; being too sociable, rather than being serious about their own and others' problems; not staying for the after-group session, which immediately follows each regular session and is led by one of my assistant therapists after I leave the regular group session; and "subgrouping," or rudely interrupting others when the group is going on. I usually intervene soon after these issues arise, and raise the issue either with the individual who is interfering with the group process or with the group as a whole.

My strategy of intervention is usually direct and often confrontational. Thus, I may say, "Jim, you always bring up your own problems in group and seem to have no trouble speaking about them. But I rarely hear you say anything to the other group members about their problems. When you sit there silently while the rest of us are speaking to one of the group members, I suspect that you are saying quite a lot to yourself that you are not saying to the group. Am I right about this? And if I am, what are you telling yourself to *stop* yourself from speaking up to the others?"

A more general intervention will also usually be direct and will go something like this: "Several of you recently are not doing your agreed-upon homework or are doing it very sloppily. Let's discuss this right now and see if I am observing this correctly and, if so, what can we do about it to see that the homework assignments are more useful and to arrange that you tend to follow them more often and more thoroughly."

If the group process is going well and the members are fairly consistently bringing up and working on their problems, both in the group and outside the group, my interventions are relatively few in regard to the group process. But I frequently question, challenge, advise, and confront members about their individual problems. I am an active teacher, confronter, persuader, encourager, and homework suggester, and I usually talk more than any of the other members during a given session. I try to make sure, however, that I do not give long lectures or hold the floor too long. My questions and comments, therefore, are usually frequent but brief.

Although I can easily run one of my groups by myself, without any assistance, because the Institute for Rational-Emotive Therapy in New York is a training institute and because we want all of our trainees to be able to lead a group by themselves, I am usually assisted by one of our trainees, a Fellow or Intern of the Institute. This assistant leader is with me and the group for the first hour and a half of each session and takes over the group by himself or herself for the after-group, which consists of another 45 minutes. The assistant leader is also trained to make active-directive interventions, but not to hog the floor at any one time, and to encourage the other members to keep making interventions, too. A few of the members in each group usually become quite vocal and adept at making interventions, but I tactfully correct them if they seem to go too far off base. The assistant leader and I particularly go after the nonintervening members and keep encouraging them to speak up more and more about other people's problems. If they are recalcitrant or resistant in this respect, we fairly often give them the assignment of speaking up a minimum of three times in each session about *others'* issues.

I keep showing the members how their behavior in group often—but by no means always—mirrors their behaviors and problems outside the group. Thus, if one member speaks sharply to another member, I may say, "Mary, you seem to be angry right now at Joan. Are you just objecting to her behavior, with which you may disagree? Or are you, as I seem to hear you doing, damning *her* for exhibiting that *behavior?*" If Mary acknowledges her anger at Joan, I (and the other members) may then ask, "What are you telling yourself right now to make yourself angry? What is your Jehovian *demand* on Joan?" If Mary denies that she is angrily carping at Joan, I may then ask the rest of the group, "What do you think and feel about Mary's reactions to Joan? Am I just inventing her anger or do you sense it, too?"

We then get the group reactions to Mary; and if the group agrees that she probably is quite angry at Joan, we go back to the question: "What are you telling yourself right now to *make* yourself angry?" The others and I will also try to get Mary to see that she is making the same kind of demands about those at whom she is angry as she is now making about Joan in the group.

Again, if Ted only offers practical advice to the other members and never helps them to see and to dispute their self-defeating philosophies by which they are upsetting themselves, I, my assistant therapist, or one of the group members may say to him, "Look, Ted, you just ignored Harold's perfectionist demands that are making him refuse to work on the novel he is trying to write, and, instead, you only offered him some practical advice on how to take a writing course. You often seem to do this same kind of thing in group. Now isn't it likely that in your own life you don't look for and dispute your irrational beliefs and that you mainly look for practical ways of your acting better *with* those irrationalities, so that you do not have to tackle them and give them up?"

Working with Difficult Group Members

One kind of difficult group member is the one who interferes with the group process, such as Mel, who interrupted others, indicated that they were pretty worthless for not changing their ways, and often monopolized the group. Other members and I pointed this out to him several times, but he persisted in his disruptive behavior. So we insisted that he stop and consider what he was telling himself when, for example, he interrupted others.

His main musturbatory beliefs appeared to be (1) "I *must* get in what I have to say immediately, or else I might lose it and never get to say it, and that would be *awful!*" and (2) "If I don't make a more brilliant statement to the group than any of the others makes, I am an inadequate person and I might as well shut my mouth and say nothing at all!" We showed Mel how to dispute and change these ideas to *preferences,* but not *necessities,* that he speak and be heard and that he make fine contributions in group. We also gave him the homework assignment of watching his interrupting tendencies and forcing himself for a while to speak up in group only after he had given some other member the choice of speaking up first. After several more sessions, he had distinctly improved his interruptive tendencies, and reported that he was doing the same thing in his group participations and individual conversations outside the group.

Another difficult type of member is the one who rarely completes the homework assignment he has agreed to do, or else completes it occasionally and sloppily. I (and other group members) then ask him to look for the irrational ideas that he is overtly or tacitly holding to block his doing these assignments, such as: "It's hard to do this goddamned assignment; in fact, it's *too* hard and it *shouldn't* be that hard!

I can get away with improving myself *without* doing it, even though other people have to do their homework to change. Screw it, I won't do it !" We keep after this member to look at the beliefs he holds to block his doing the homework; to make a list of the disadvantages of not doing it and to go over this list at least five times every day; to dispute his irrational beliefs strongly and forcefully; to keep telling himself rational coping self-statements in their stead; to use rational emotive imagery to make himself feel sorry and displeased, but not horrified and rebellious, about having to do the homework; to reinforce himself whenever he does it, and perhaps to also penalize himself when he doesn't do it; and to use other suitable methods of REBT to undercut his dysfunctional thinking, feeling, and behaving about doing the homework.

Another type of difficult group member is the one who is overly passive, polite, and nonparticipative. I usually do nothing about such a member until she has been in the group for several weeks and has had a chance to acclimate herself to its procedures and to some of the principles of REBT. But then I directly question her about her passivity and lack of participation. If she acknowledges these behaviors, I encourage her to look at her blocking thoughts and actively to dispute them. Thus, one member, Josephine, kept telling herself, just before she thought of speaking up in group, "What if I say something stupid! They'll all laugh at me! I'll be an utter fool! They are all brighter than I and know much better how to use REBT. I'll *never* be able to say something intelligent or to be helpful to the other group members. I'd better quit group and only go for individual therapy where it is much easier for me to speak up, because I only have to talk about myself and don't have to help others with their problems."

In this case, the group and I did what we usually do: we disputed Josephine's unrealistic attributions and inferences and showed her that she wouldn't necessarily say something stupid; that the group might well not laugh at her even if she did; that all the members were not necessarily brighter than she; and that if she kept trying, she most probably would be able to say something intelligent and to be helpful to the other members. As usual, however, we went beyond this— as we almost always do in REBT—by showing Josephine, more elegantly, that even if the worst happened, even if she did say something stupid, even if she was laughed at by the group, even if all the others were brighter than she, and even if she never was able to say something intelligent or to be helpful to the others, she still would never be an inadequate or rotten person, but would only be a person who was now behaving poorly and who could always accept and respect herself while remaining unenthusiastic about some of her traits and behaviors.

This is what we usually try to achieve with difficult clients who continually down and damn themselves and who steadily, therefore, feel depressed, panicked, and worthless. The group members and I persist in showing her that we accept her as a fallible human, and that she can learn to consistently do the same for herself. REBT group therapy, like REBT individual therapy, is particularly oriented toward helping all clients give themselves unconditional self-acceptance; that is, to reject and to try to change many of their dysfunctional behaviors but always—yes, always!—to accept themselves as humans. Yes, *whether or not* they perform well and *whether or not* they are approved or loved by significant others.

This is one of the cardinal views of REBT; and one that often— though, of course, not always—works well with difficult clients. This aspect of REBT is probably more effective in group than in individual therapy, because all the members of the group are taught to accept both themselves and others unconditionally; so that when an arrant self-denigrator comes to group, she is not only accepted unconditionally by the therapist (who is especially trained to do this kind of accepting) but is almost always also accepted by the other group members, thus encouraging and abetting her unconditionally to accept herself.

Activity of the Therapist and Group Members

In cognitive-behavioral therapy in general and in REBT group therapy in particular, the activity level of the therapist tends to be high. I am a teacher, who often shows my clients how they upset themselves and what they can do to change, but I also keep encouraging and pushing them to change. The romantic view in therapy is that if clients are provided with a trusting and accepting atmosphere they have considerable ability to change, and will healthfully use this ability to get themselves to grow and develop. I take the more realistic view that they *can* but that they often *won't* choose to modify their thoughts, feelings, and behaviors unless I actively and directively push them to do so. Consequently, as noted previously in this chapter, I speak more than any other group member during each session; I purposely and purposively lead the group in "healthy" rather than "unhealthy" directions; and I keep each session going in an organized, no-nonsense, presumably efficient way. I try to make sure that no one is neglected during each session; that no one monopolizes the group; and that sidetracking into chit-chat, empty discussion, bombast, endless philosophizing, and other modes of problem avoidance is minimized.

As leader, I try to maximize honest revealing of feelings, cutting through defensiveness, getting to members' core dysfunctional philosophies, Disputing of these philosophies, acceptance of present discomfort, and the carrying out of difficult in-group and out-of-group experiential and behavioral assignments. For example, I (or the other members) may suggest that Sam, an unusually shy person, go around the room and start a conversation with every member who is present. I will then direct Sam to do so, will encourage him to keep going around the room, will ask him about his feelings as he does so, will get him to look at what he is thinking to create these feelings, will ask the other members for the reactions to his overtures, and will lead a general discussion on what has just transpired and how Sam and other members can gain from this exercise. Once, when we did this exercise with an exceptionally shy man, he not only became very much more active in group from that session onward, but also, for the first time in his life, began to approach people in his neighborhood bar, where previously he had always waited for them to approach him. He noted that my actively persuading him and the group to participate in this encouraging exercise was a real turning point in his life.

The activity level of most of the members of my five weekly groups is usually quite high, not only in the expressing of their feelings and ideas, but in their disputing other members' self-defeating beliefs and helping them with their problem-solving.

In the section that follows, I provide a case example of how one particular client benefited from her participation in an REBT group.

CASE PRESENTATION OF A GROUP CLIENT

Barbara came to group because of her business and social unassertiveness. A 36-year-old secretary, she had always worked below her potential level because she nicely followed her supervisor's instructions but never took any initiative herself. She therefore failed to become a supervisor or office manager herself, although she definitely seemed to have the ability to do that kind of work. She married at the age of 21 and stayed with her alcoholic and irresponsible husband for 8 years because of her horror of being alone. Although quite attractive, she practically never went to singles functions, but stayed in her apartment by herself most of the time, because she was afraid to socialize and be rejected by any "good" men she might meet. She felt that she had "nothing really to offer," except to an inferior male. So she only, occasionally, dated unsuccessful, inadequate men whom she found "safe" but too boring to stay with for any length of time. She had one close woman friend, Selma, who—like herself—was painfully shy and who only socialized with Barbara.

At first, Barbara talked freely enough about herself in group, especially about her unassertiveness at work and about her accompanying depression. But she would only give practical advice to other group members and never found or Disputed their irrational Beliefs. When asked about this in group, she said that she did not know how to do REBT well enough to do good Disputation, even though she had read several REBT self-help books and pamphlets.

To show Barbara that she *was* able to do Disputing adequately, she was asked to fill out the RET Self-Help Form (Sichel & Ellis, 1984), first, about one of her own problems; and, second, about another group member's unassertiveness with her husband. When Barbara did very well on these homework assignments and admitted that she could do adequate REBT Disputation, she was encouraged to do live Disputing of some other group members' irrational Beliefs during several group sessions, and was again shown that she could do this well. After several weeks, she became one of the group's most frequent and persistent Disputers, and began to obviously enjoy the process. She also spontaneously began, outside of therapy, to teach REBT to her shy friend, Selma, and to considerably help Selma with some of her neurotic difficulties.

For several months, Barbara complained and put herself down for her unassertiveness with her supervisor at work. She saw that it stemmed from her dire need for this woman's approval, but did nothing to change her love slobbism or to act more assertively. After doing some assertiveness-training role-playing in group, and after being urged by all the other members to follow it up on the outside, she forced herself to speak up at work. Doing so, she soon arranged to get the promise of a raise in pay; also arranged to come in an hour earlier and to leave work earlier on Tuesdays and Thursdays, so that she could take a special word-processing course; and was able to ask for a few other favors at work that she had been terrified to request for more than 2 years. Both Barbara and the group were delighted with her increased assertiveness, and she was encouraged to look for a better job—which, after 4 months, she finally attained.

Barbara's social anxiety proved more difficult to tackle than her unassertiveness at work, because she invented innumerable excuses to avoid going to singles affairs and to respond appropriately to males who tried to approach her at church, when she walked her dog, and at the other few "safe" activities in which she allowed herself to participate. She even refused to try a date with an eligible male cousin of Selma, who talked to this cousin and got him interested in seeing Barbara. She was sure that he would lose all interest in her if they actually met, and was terrified that he might have sex with her because he was only interested in her body and would then never want to see her again. She broke two tentative dates with him and perpetuated her perfect record of not having a single date in 3 years.

The group and I tried several REBT techniques to help Barbara overcome her extreme fears of rejection. We used referenting, and had her list many disadvantages of being socially reclusive and read these over many times to sink them into her consciousness. We tried to help her model herself after other group members who were overcoming their social shyness. We had her say several forceful coping statements to herself a number of times—such as, "I *can* find some males who will like me for more than my body! And if any of them have sex with me and then reject me, that means something about *them* but never, never proves that *I* am an inadequate person!"

The group showed Barbara how to use rational-emotive imagery by imagining that she did get rejected by one of the few men she really liked, letting herself feel very depressed and self-hating about this rejection, and then working on herself until she only felt quite sorry and disappointed but *not* depressed. Most of all, the group and I gave Barbara unconditional acceptance and showed her, by our attitude, tone, and manner, that we always accepted *her*, as a person, even when she failed to work on herself, when she sabotaged our suggestions, and when she made up poor excuses for staying in her rut. In addition, of course, we consistently and vigorously taught her unconditional self-acceptance (USA)—that is, fully to accept *herself* no matter how badly, foolishly, and self-defeating she often *acted*. After going over this important point many times, Barbara improved greatly at refusing to blame herself for her mistakes and failures; and she also helped talk several other group members into unconditionally accepting themselves even when they acted quite foolishly.

All this REBT work, by Barbara and by her therapy group, eventually began to pay off. After attending group regularly for 5 months, she finally agreed to do the paradoxical homework assignment of going to a dance and making sure that she got at least three rejections by suitable males. She was enormously afraid, at first, to carry out this assignment, and for several weeks copped out on doing it. But she finally painfully forced herself to go to a "safe" church dance and get three men to refuse to dance with her. After the first refusal, she almost ran shamefully back home. But she made herself stay, to her surprise got several acceptances, and just barely, by the end of the evening, got her required three rejections. She was elated with her social assertiveness—and so were the other members of her group.

From then onward, Barbara's battle with herself went almost swimmingly smoothly. She dated with increasing frequency, and was disappointed, but not depressed, when the "good" men she occasionally met didn't turn out to be suitable for a long-term relationship. She became active in other ways—especially by participating in a regular discussion group. She became even more active in her therapy group and was voted, in one of the exercises we did, as being the most helpful member. She got a job as an office manager, liked it very much, and did more socializing at the new office in a few weeks than she had previously done in any of the previous jobs that she had kept for years.

After being in group for a little over a year, Barbara decided to leave, partly because she now had so many other things to do in the evening that spending several hours once a week traveling to and from and being in group was getting too exhausting. But she mainly felt that she had achieved her goals of socializing better and becoming more assertive, and that she could continue therapy with intermittent individual sessions. She was still at times socially anxious, but was practically never severely depressed as she had often been previously.

The group members were very sorry to see Barbara leave and hoped she would invite them to her future wedding, which they were sure would not be too far away. Several of them continued to have personal friendships with her for quite a while after she left group. She herself was very happy about her group experience, remarked that she would have never benefited so much with just individual therapy sessions, and kept referring her friends and business associates to the Institute, particularly for group therapy.

Not every member of my groups, of course, makes the dramatic and steady progress that Barbara made, and some take 2 or 3 years of participation before they do significantly improve. But if people really work at it, and keep using REBT in group as well as in their outside lives, a large percentage of them make notable gains, minimize their anxiety, depression, and rage, and begin to lead much more self-actualized lives.

CONCLUSION

Rational emotive behavior and cognitive behavior therapy are partly indigenous to most group therapy, because when several people regularly meet together with a leader in order to work on their psychological problems, they almost always talk about their thoughts, feelings, and behaviors and try to help each other change their cognitions, emotions, and actions. Moreover, they usually give advice to each other, show how others' behavior had better be changed outside the group, and check to see if their homework suggestions are actually being carried out. Again, they normally interact with each other in the group itself, comment on each other's in-group behaviors, and give themselves practice in changing some of their dysfunctional interactions.

Even, then, when a therapy group tries to follow a somewhat narrow theory of psychotherapy—for example, a psychoanalytic or a Jungian orientation—it tends to be much wider-ranging in its actions than in its theory, and often takes on a surprisingly eclectic approach (Bennett, 1984; Yalom, 1985). The advantage of REBT group therapy is that it very consciously deals with members as people who think, feel, *and* act; who get disturbed, or *make* themselves disturbed, in all three interacting ways; and who, therefore, had better consciously see how they largely *construct* their dysfunctioning and how they can *re*construct and improve their patterns of living (Ellis, 1991; Ellis & Dryden, 1996).

REBT and CBT group therapy, moreover, in principle accept the fact that humans are social animals and live interpersonally and in groups. It is therefore desirable, though not absolutely necessary, that they work out their cognitive-emotive-behavioral problems together as well as in individual therapy. Group work also covers a wide variety of goals and problems. Thus, therapy groups may be homogeneous— e.g., all the members may be involved in skill training, overcoming alcoholism, or overcoming procrastination—or may be heterogeneous—e.g., the group may include several kinds of disturbed people. While one specific type of treatment is unlikely to be helpful to members of all these different kinds of groups, REBT includes so many different kinds of techniques that it can fairly easily be adapted to almost any kind of group process. With the use of group treatment, more opportunity for learning positive and unlearning self-defeating behavior is provided than one therapist can provide in individual therapy and than one group therapist can provide in a one-sided form of group process (Ellis, 1962, 1982, 1990; Lazarus, 1968).

From a research standpoint, rational emotive behavioral group therapy offers unique possibilities for exploring the effectiveness of group techniques. For it always includes many specific procedures— such as the Disputing of dysfunctional attitudes, the disclosure of "shameful" feelings, and the assigning of homework activities—and each of these methods can be used and not used in controlled experiments, to determine how effective or ineffective each of them is in different kinds of groups and settings. If enough of this kind of experimentation is done, the wide variety of methods now used in REBT (and in CBT) may eventually be pared down to a relatively few effective ones.

For reasons such as these, then, I think that REBT and CBT group therapy will, first, become more popular as the years go by and, second, be increasingly incorporated into or merged with many of the other modes of group treatment. At the same time, cognitive-behavioral group and individual therapy will continue to change as the entire field of psychotherapy grows and develops. Some of its more popular present-day methods will wane and other methods, including some not yet invented, will flourish. Like its sister, behavior therapy, and unlike many of today's other treatment methods, CBT favors scientific experimentation, and already has led to literally hundreds of controlled studies (Hollon & Beck, 1994; Lyons & Woods, 1991). If this characteristic continues, as I predict it will, REBT and CBT will continue to change and develop.

REFERENCES

Ansbacher, H. L., & Ansbacher, R. (1956). *The individual psychology of Alfred Adler.* New York: Basic.

Bandura, A. (1986). *Social foundations of thought and action: A social cognition theory.* Englewood Cliffs, NJ: Prentice-Hall.

Bennett, T. S. (1984). Group psychotherapy. In R. Corsini (Ed.), *Encyclopedia of psychology* (Vol. 2) (pp. 81–82). New York: Wiley.

Bernard, M. E. (Ed.). (1991). *Using rational-emotive therapy effectively: A practitioner's guide.* New York: Plenum.

Bernard, M. E. (1993). *Staying rational in an irrational world.* New York: Carol Publishing.

Bernard, M. E., & Wolfe, J. L. (Eds.). (1993). *The RET resource book for practitioners.* New York: Institute for Rational-Emotive Therapy.

Corsini, R. J. (1957). *Methods of group psychotherapy.* New York: McGraw-Hill.

Danysh, J. (1974). *Stop without quitting.* San Francisco: International Society for General Semantics.

Dryden, W. (1994). *Progress in rational emotive behaviour therapy.* London: Whurr.

Dryden, W., Backx, W., & Ellis, A. (1987). Problems in living: The Friday night workshop. In W. Dryden (Ed.), *Current issues in rational-emotive therapy* (pp. 154–170). London and New York: Croom Helm.

Dryden, W., & DiGiuseppe, R. (1990). *A primer on rational-emotive therapy.* Champaign, IL: Research Press.

Ellis, A. (1957). *How to live with a neurotic: At home and at work.* New York: Crown. Rev. ed., Hollywood, CA: Wilshire Books, 1975.

Ellis, A. (1962). *Reason and emotion in psychotherapy.* Secaucus, NJ: Citadel.

Ellis, A. (1968). Is psychoanalysis harmful? *Psychiatric Opinion, 5,* 16–25.

Ellis, A. (1969a). A cognitive approach to behavior therapy. *International Journal of Psychiatry, 8,* 896–900.

Ellis, A. (1969b). A weekend of rational encounter. *Rational Living, 4,* 1–8. Reprinted in A. Ellis & W. Dryden, *The practice of rational-emotive therapy* (pp.180–191). New York: Springer, 1987.

Ellis, A. (1973). *Humanistic psychotherapy: The rational-emotive approach.* New York: McGraw-Hill.

Ellis, A. (1975). *How to live with a neurotic: At home and at work.* (Rev. ed.). Hollywood, CA: Wilshire Books.

Ellis, A. (1976). *Sex and the liberated man.* Secaucus, NJ: Lyle Stuart.

Ellis, A. (1977a). Fun as psychotherapy. *Rational Living, 12,* 2–6. Also: Cassette recording. New York: Institute for Rational-Emotive Therapy.

Ellis, A. (1977b). *A garland of rational humorous songs* (Cassette recording and songbook). New York: Institute for Rational-Emotive Therapy.

Ellis, A. (1977c). Skill training in counseling and psychotherapy. *Canadian Counsellor, 12,* 30–35.

Ellis, A. (1982). Rational-emotive group therapy. In G. M. Gazda (Ed.), *Basic approaches to group psychotherapy and group counseling,* 3rd ed. (pp. 381–412). Springfield, IL: Thomas.

Ellis, A. (1985). *Overcoming resistance: Rational-emotive therapy with difficult clients.* New York: Springer.

Ellis, A. (1988). *How to stubbornly refuse to make yourself miserable about anything—yes, anything!* Secaucus, NJ: Lyle Stuart.

Ellis, A. (1990). Rational-emotive therapy. In I. L. Kutash & A. Wolfe (Eds.), *The group psychotherapist's handbook* (pp. 295–315). New York: Columbia University.

Ellis, A. (1991). Achieving self-actualization. *Journal of Social Behavior and Personality, 6,* 1–18.

Ellis, A. (1992). Group rational-emotive and cognitive-behavioral therapy. *International Journal of Group Psychotherapy, 42,* 63–80.

Ellis, A. (1993). Rational emotive imagery: RET version. In M. E. Bernard & J. L. Wolfe (Eds.), *The RET source book for practitioners* (pp. II–8–II–10). New York: Institute for Rational-Emotive Therapy.

Ellis, A. (1994). Post-traumatic stress disorder (PTSD) in rape victims: A rational emotive behavioral theory. *Journal of Rational-Emotive and Cognitive-Behavior Therapy, 12,* 3–25.

Ellis, A., & Abrahms, E. (1978). *Brief psychotherapy in medical and health practice.* New York: Springer.

Ellis, A., & Abrams, M. (1994). *How to cope with a fatal illness.* New York: Barricade Books.

Ellis, A., Abrams, M., & Dengelegi, L. (1992). *The art and science of rational eating.* New York: Barricade Books.

Ellis, A., & Dryden, W. (1996). *The clinical practice of rational emotive behavior therapy.* New York: Springer.

Ellis, A., & Grieger, R. (Eds.). (1977). *Handbook of rational-emotive therapy* (Vol. 1). New York: Springer.

Ellis, A., & Grieger, R. (Eds.). (1986). *Handbook of rational-emotive therapy* (Vol. 2). New York: Springer.

Ellis, A., & Harper, R. A. (1961). *A guide to successful marriage.* North Hollywood, CA: Wilshire Books.

Ellis, A., & Harper, R. A. (1975). *A new guide to rational living.* North Hollywood, CA: Wilshire Books.

Ellis, A., & Lange, A. (1994). *How to keep people from pushing your buttons.* New York: Carol Publishing.

Ellis, A., McInerney, J. F., DiGiuseppe, R., & Yeager, R. (1988). *Rational-emotive therapy with alcoholics and substance abusers.* Needham, MA: Allyn & Bacon.

Ellis, A., Sichel, J., Leaf, R. C., & Mass, R. (1989). Countering perfectionism in research on clinical practice. I: Surveying rationality changes after a single intensive RET intervention. *Journal of Rational-Emotive & Cognitive-Behavior Therapy, 7,* 197–218.

Ellis, A., & Velten, E. (1992). *When AA doesn't work: Rational steps to quitting alcohol.* New York: Barricade Books.

Franklin, R. (1993). *Overcoming the myth of self-worth.* Appleton, WI: Focus Press.

Hauck, P. A. (1992). *Overcoming the rating game: Beyond self-love — beyond self-esteem.* Louisville, KY: Westminster/Jon Knox.

Hollon, S. D., & Beck, A. T. (1994). Cognitive and behavioral therapies. In S. L. Garfield & A. E. Bergin (Eds.), *Handbook of psychotherapy and behavioral change,* 4th ed. New York: Wiley.

Institute for Rational-Emotive Therapy (1994, Spring). *Catalogue.* New York: Author.

Lazarus, A. A. (1968). Behavior therapy in groups. In G. M. Gazda (Ed.), *Basic approaches to group psychotherapy and group counseling* (pp. 149–175). Springfield, IL: Charles C. Thomas.

Losoncy, L. E. (1980). *You can do it: How to encourage yourself.* Englewood Cliffs, NJ: Prentice-Hall.

Lyons, L. C., & Woods, P. J. (1991). The efficacy of rational-emotive therapy: A quantitative review of the outcome research. *Clinical Psychology Review, 11,* 357–369.

Marlatt, G. A., & Gordon, J. R. (Eds.). (1989). *Relapse prevention: Maintenance strategies in the treatment of addictive behaviors.* New York: Guilford.

Maultsby, M. C., Jr. (1971). Rational emotive imagery. *Rational Living, 6,* 24–27.

Maultsby, M. C., Jr., & Ellis, A. (1974). *Technique for using rational-emotive imagery.* New York: Institute for Rational-Emotive Therapy.

Mills, D. (1993). *Overcoming self-esteem.* New York: Institute for Rational-Emotive Therapy.

Moore, R. H. (1993). Traumatic incident reduction. In W. Dryden & L. K. Hill (Eds.), *Innovations in rational-emotive therapy* (pp. 116–159). Newbury Park, CA: Sage.

Moreno, J. L. (1990). *The essential J.L. Moreno.* New York: Springer.

Rogers, C. R. (1961). *On becoming a person.* Boston: Houghton-Mifflin.

Rogers, C. R. (1980). *A way of being.* Boston: Houghton-Mifflin.

Rose, S. D. (1980). *Casebook in group therapy: A behavioral-cognitive approach.* Englewood Cliffs, NJ: Prentice-Hall.

Sichel, J., & Ellis, A. (1984). *RET self-help form.* New York: Institute for Rational-Emotive Therapy.

Upper, D., & Rose, S. (Eds.). *Behavioral group therapy.* Champaign, IL: Research Press.

Walen, S., DiGiuseppe, R., & Dryden, W. (1992). *A practitioner's guide to rational-emotive therapy.* New York: Oxford University Press.

Yalom, I. D. (1985). *The theory and practice of group psychotherapy,* 3rd ed. New York: Basic Books.

Yankura, J., & Dryden, W. (1990). *Doing RET: Albert Ellis in action.* New York: Springer.

CHAPTER 7

Conclusion

Joseph Yankura and Windy Dryden

After giving due consideration to the matter, we decided to conclude this casebook with a compilation of resources for readers who wish to learn more about applications of REBT. What follows is an annotated bibliography containing information on journal articles, books, and chapters which illustrate (through case descriptions and, in numerous instances, actual session transcript material) how REBT can be used to treat various psychological problems and enhance healthy functioning. We have also listed a number of videotapes which show several prominent REBT practitioners working "live" with clients having particular sorts of clinical problems. These tapes can be ordered directly from the Institute for Rational-Emotive Therapy in New York City, but are available only to mental health professionals. Most of the books we list can also be ordered from the Institute; we have marked these with an asterisk. At the end of this chapter, for readers' convenience, we provide telephone and fax numbers (as well as a World Wide Web address) which can be used for ordering Institute materials.

In choosing the resources to include in this annotated bibliography, we kept several criteria in mind. First, we wanted to include materials of fairly recent vintage that would represent REBT as it is currently practiced. Second, we wanted to provide sources that *illustrate* REBT's actual application to a given problem or issue through case descriptions and/or session transcript material. Thus, we have not included references for REBT treatment outcome studies, as such empirical reports typically do not detail what transpires between therapist and client during treatment. Finally, we tried to identify a number of sources which show REBT's implementation with problems and issues not covered by the our casebooks. You will find that almost all of the references listed below meet at least two of these three standards. We hope that you find them useful!

Articles

Ellis, A. (1984). How to deal with your most difficult client—you. *Psychotherapy in Private Practice, 2,* 25–35.

Although not focused on presenting case material, this article is noteworthy because it describes irrational beliefs which may block therapists from functioning effectively in their professional roles. Ellis briefly describes fifteen techniques that therapists can use to challenge and surrender their unhelpful beliefs.

Ellis, A. (1984). Treating the abrasive client with rational-emotive therapy (RET). *The Psychotherapy Patient, 1,* 21–25.

In this paper, Ellis illustrates the REBT approach to dealing with hostile clients by describing his work with a 25-year-old woman whom he refers to as "Abrasa." While this client was largely unresponsive to attempts to help her dispute her own irrational beliefs, she was receptive to engaging in "rational proselytizing," and gradually began to think more rationally as she worked at talking others out of their irrationalities.

Ellis, A. (1990). Treating the widowed client with rational-emotive therapy (RET). *The Psychotherapy Patient, 6,* 105–111.

In this article, Ellis notes that in response to the death of a spouse, many widows make themselves unnecessarily and self-defeatingly depressed as well as appropriately sad and grieving. He describes how he employed REBT cognitive, emotive, and behavioral methods to help Sarah, a 68-year-old widow, defeat her depression and take a number of rational, life-enhancing risks.

Ellis, A. (1991). Rational-emotive treatment of simple phobias. *Psychotherapy, 28,* 452–456.

The case of a 24-year-old man is used to illustrate how REBT deploys cognitive, emotive, and behavioral techniques to help clients with simple phobias change their musturbatory philosophies, feel and act against the phobia, and ultimately overcome it. The client's anxiety about having the phobia was also addressed and treated.

Ellis, A. (1994). Post-traumatic stress disorder (PTSD): A rational emotive behavioral theory. *Journal of Rational-Emotive and Cognitive-Behavior Therapy, 12,* 3–25.

Ellis presents an REBT perspective on PTSD, compares REBT with other forms of cognitive-behavior therapy, and provides a case example of a 25-year-old woman who was molested in early adolescence.

Ellis, A. (1994). The treatment of borderline personalities with rational emotive behavior therapy. *Journal of Rational-Emotive and Cognitive-Behavior Therapy, 12,* 101–119.

Ellis describes his REBT conceptualization of borderline personality disorder (BPD) and presents the case of Rona, a 25-year-old woman with an MBA who worked as a bookkeeper in a small office. While important improvements in Rona's functioning are reported, Ellis acknowledges that clients with BPD tend to make limited gains in therapy.

Malkinson, R. (1996). Cognitive behavioral grief therapy. *Journal of Rational-Emotive and Cognitive-Behavior Therapy, 14,* 155–171.

The author proposes a distinction between functional and dysfunctional bereavement processes, and recommends detailed assessment of the likely irrational beliefs that may block a healthier course of grief. Case illustrations are presented.

Vernon, A. (1990). The school psychologist's role in preventative education: Applications of rational-emotive education. *School Psychology Review, 19,* 322–330.

This article is of note because it describes an alternative application of rational-emotive concepts in a non-clinical setting. Specifically, it discusses rational-emotive education (REE) and the role of the school psychologist in introducing this intervention to teachers interested in employing mental health prevention programs.

Wood, P. J., & Grieger, R. M. (1993). Bulimia: A case study with mediating cognitions and notes on a cognitive-behavioral analysis of eating disorders. *Journal of Rational-Emotive and Cognitive-Behavior Therapy, 11,* 159–172.

The authors describe the treatment of a 19-year-old bulimic woman who was shown how to dispute her irrational beliefs and replace them with more rational, self-enhancing alternatives. She was also trained in a cognitive-behavioral weight control program that emphasized quality and regularity of food intake. The client resumed a normal eating pattern and had not experienced any bulimic regression 15 months after the end of treatment.

Books

* Dryden, W. (1990). *Dealing with anger problems: Rational-emotive therapeutic interventions.* Sarasota, FL: Professional Resource Exchange.

In this concise book, Dryden first provides necessary background material on REBT and then details the ten steps of the rational-emotive treatment sequence as they would apply when dealing with clients' anger problems. These steps are illustrated with verbatim excerpts from an actual case.

* Dryden, W., & DiGiuseppe, R. (1990). *A primer on rational-emotive therapy.* Champaign, IL: Research Press.

The goal of this book is to provide readers with a concise introduction to the structured steps of the rational-emotive treatment sequence. The final section uses session dialogue between therapist and client to illustrate how this sequence is actually deployed. Dryden works with a 26-year-old woman experiencing emotional problems and social avoidance related to her fiance's breaking off with her. This book is a "must" for those wishing to learn the essentials of implementing REBT.

*   Dryden, W., & Hill, L. K. (Eds.) (1993). *Innovations in rational-emotive therapy*. Newbury Park, CA: Sage.

This book contains useful chapters on REBT approaches to treating: (1) adult children of alcoholics; (2) pathological gambling; (3) chronic pain; (4) post-traumatic stress disorder; (5) performance anxiety; and (6) the fear of flying. The authors of the various chapters utilize case examples and/or transcript material to illustrate REBT's deployment with the problem area under review.

*   Dryden, W., & Yankura, J. (1992). *Daring to be myself: A case study in rational-emotive therapy*. Buckingham: Open University Press.

This book documents a complete course of rational-emotive treatment through extensive transcript material and commentary by the authors. It shows how Windy Dryden helped his client, Sarah, to overcome her feelings of depression, guilt, and shame, and become more assertive.

Ellis, A. (Ed.) (1971). *Growth through reason: Verbatim cases in rational-emotive therapy*. Palo Alto, CA: Science and Behavior Books.

Although published 25 years ago, this book may be of interest because it shows how six different therapists employ the rational-emotive approach to treatment with a variety of clients. Extensive session transcript material, with commentary, is used throughout the book.

*   Ellis, A., McInerney, J. F., DiGiuseppe, R., & Yeager, R. J. (1988). *Rational-emotive therapy with alcoholics and substance abusers*. Oxford, England: Pergamon Press.

While this volume does not include actual case material, it provides a useful description of a rational-emotive theory of addiction and a compendium of techniques for use with alcoholics and substance abusers.

*   Ellis, A., Sichel, J. L., Yeager, R. J., DiMattia, D. J., & DiGiuseppe, R. (1989). *Rational-emotive couples therapy*. Elmsford, NY: Pergamon.

The authors provide a comprehensive overview of REBT's application to couples' problems, and present session transcript material in separate chapters dealing with sexual problems and jealousy.

* Huber, C. H., & Baruth, L. G. (1989). *Rational-emotive family therapy: A systems perspective.* New York: Springer.

In the first two sections of this book, the authors discuss the theoretical foundations and therapeutic implications of a rational-emotive approach to family therapy. In the third section they deal with clinical applications and present two case studies which include session transcript material.

* Yankura, J., & Dryden, W. (1990). *Doing RET: Albert Ellis in action.* New York: Springer.

This book provides a comprehensive overview of how Albert Ellis actually implements the form of psychotherapy he originated. While it doesn't focus on describing applications of REBT to particular clinical problems, it may be of interest to casebook readers because of the considerable amount of session transcript material it presents. It also includes a chapter in which prior clients of Ellis confide their reactions to his therapy.

Chapters

"A client's view of rational-emotive counselling." In W. Dryden & J. Yankura (1993). *Counselling individuals: A rational-emotive handbook* (2nd ed.) (pp. 243–256). London: Whurr.

In this chapter, one of Windy Dryden's former clients describes (in her own words) her REBT treatment experience. She was troubled by "inappropriate" obsessive thoughts of a sexual nature, and suffered from guilt, shame, depression, and behavioral avoidance with respect to these thoughts. By treatment's end, she reports that she had made significant progress in minimizing her presenting symptoms.

Dryden, W. (1987). Theoretically-consistent eclecticism: Humanizing a computer "addict." In J. C. Norcross (Ed.), *Casebook of eclectic psychotherapy* (pp. 221–237). New York: Brunner/Mazel.

In this very interesting chapter, Dryden illustrates how he employed a stance of "theoretically-consistent eclecticism" in his work with Eric, a 31-year-old computer programmer. While consistently operating from a rational-emotive theoretical base, Dryden employed a number of methods derived from alternative approaches to therapy. By the end of treatment, Eric, who had been socially isolated and out of touch with his emotional life, was more comfortable with experiencing and expressing feelings and had become more socially active.

Dryden, W. (1991). A note on how I used RET to overcome my emotional problems. In W. Dryden (Ed.), *Reason and therapeutic change* (pp. 301–303). London: Whurr.

Dryden describes how he employed REBT methods (largely in a self-help fashion) to deal with his stammering problem, a period of depression he experienced, and anger about being rejected by a training program to which he had applied. Of note, he reports that three separate experiences as a client in psychoanalytic psychotherapy did little to relieve his mild depression. On the other hand, REBT self-help techniques proved quite effective.

Dryden, W., & Backx, W. (1987). Problems in living: The Friday night workshop. In W. Dryden (Ed.), *Current issues in rational-emotive therapy* (pp. 154–170). New York: Croom Helm.

For the past 30 years or so, Albert Ellis has provided live demonstrations of REBT at his Friday evening workshop at the Institute for Rational-Emotive Therapy in New York City. This chapter describes the process of these demonstrations, and uses transcript material to illustrate how Ellis works with a "volunteer client" (in this case, the second author) from the workshop audience.

Ellis, A. (1992). Brief therapy: The rational-emotive method. In S. H. Budman, M. F. Hoyt, & S. Friedman (Eds.), *The first session in brief therapy* (pp. 36–58). New York: Guilford.

Ellis describes a brief course of REBT (3 sessions) with a 38-year-old man suffering from panic attacks. Transcript material excerpted from the initial session is presented with commentary. Gains were made during individual treatment and extended through the client's independent use of REBT psychoeducational materials and participation in REBT workshops.

Robin, M. W., & DiGiuseppe, R. (1993). Rational-emotive therapy with an avoidant personality. In K. T. Kuehlwein & H. Rosen (Eds.), *Cognitive therapies in action: Evolving innovative practice* (pp. 143–159). San Francisco, CA: Jossey-Bass.

The first author describes his work with Cynthia, a 26-year-old woman who met DSM diagnostic criteria for dysthymia, panic disorder, generalized anxiety disorder, and avoidant personality disorder. This case study reports treatment outcome data on a number of different measures, and provides support for the view that broad improvements can occur when a client's core irrational beliefs (as opposed to numerous situation-specific automatic thoughts) are targeted for change.

Videotapes

Bernard, M. E. (Therapist). (1994). *RET with children and adolescents*. New York: Institute for Rational-Emotive Therapy.

This tape shows live therapy sessions with a 10-year-old girl struggling with self-acceptance issues and a 15-year-old boy experiencing school difficulties related to feelings of anger and depression.

DiGiuseppe, R. (Therapist). (1993). *Coping with anger.* New York: Institute for Rational-Emotive Therapy.

DiGiuseppe works with a 34-year-old male experiencing anger problems at work. Attempts are made to teach the client to distinguish between anger and annoyance and the behavioral consequences of each of these emotional states. Hypothetical problematic situations that might arise on the job are presented to the client as a means for rehearsing rational coping statements and disputes.

DiGiuseppe, R. (Therapist). (1994). *Treating adult children of alcoholics.* New York: Institute for Rational-Emotive Therapy.

Provides initial and follow-up sessions with a 25-year-old woman whose belief in her own worthlessness (derived, in part, from her experiences with her alcoholic mother) contributes to self-destructive behaviors in her relationships with men.

DiMattia, D. J. (Therapist). (1993). *Overcoming depression.* New York: Institute for Rational-Emotive Therapy.

DiMattia uses REBT to help a 34-year-old man with depression, suicidal ideation, and low self-acceptance. Given the client's depression and low energy level, attempts are made to utilize approaches that will "energize" him.

Ellis, A. (Therapist). (1993). *Coping with the suicide of a loved one.* New York: Institute for Rational-Emotive Therapy.

Ellis works with a woman who witnessed her husband commit suicide 10 years ago. He attempts to help her with her feelings of guilt (about not being able to stop her husband from killing himself), anger (about being abandoned), and worry (about the effect the suicide may have on her daughter's development).

Ellis, A. (Therapist). (1994). *Dealing with addictions.* New York: Institute for Rational-Emotive Therapy.

This tape shows Ellis working with a 32-year-old polysubstance-abusing male who holds a self-defeating philosophy of low frustration tolerance and short-range hedonism.

Wolfe, J. (Therapist). (1993). *Overcoming low frustration tolerance.* New York: Institute for Rational-Emotive Therapy.

In this tape, Janet Wolfe works with a man experiencing emotional difficulties related to his recently being diagnosed as having heart disease. She narrows the focus during the session to identify an activating event of particular relevance to the client: The way his mate responds to him because of his illness. Assertiveness training and role-playing interventions are employed.

The Institute for Rational-Emotive Therapy in New York City publishes a catalogue which provides information on upcoming workshops and lectures for the public, training programs for mental health professionals, and materials which are offered for sale. To obtain this catalogue or to order materials from the Institute, you can:

Write to: Institute for Rational-Emotive Therapy
45 East 65th Street
New York, NY 10021

Phone: (800) 323–IRET (toll-free)
(212) 535–0822

Fax: (212) 249–3582

Materials can also be ordered via the Institute's World Wide Web page at www.iret.org.

Index

ABC sequence
  vs. circular causality, 101–102
  for culturally diverse clients, 45,
    51–52, 55
  for clients with disabilities, 90–91
  in family therapy, 108–111, 113–115,
    118–124
  for group clients, 137
  psychoanalysis and, 131
  in REBT, 1
Activating Events (As)
  of children and adolescents, 15–16,
    18
  client inferences about, 4
  of culturally diverse clients, 50–51
  of clients with disabilities, 74
  of family conflict, 108–111, 113–115
  modification of, 2
Active disputing in REBT groups, 136
Active-directive rehabilitation
    approach, 84–85
ADA (Americans with Disabilities Act),
    70
Adult children of alcoholics and REBT,
    170–171
Alcoholism and REBT, 167
Americans with Disabilities Act (ADA),
    70
Anger
  in children and adolescents
    continuum of, 29–30
    goal attainment and, 30
    "instant replay" technique and, 31
    payoffs of anger and, 30–31
  of culturally diverse clients, 53

  of clients with disabilities, 74–75, 82
  parental irrational beliefs and, 23
  REBT interventions for, 166, 170
Anxiety
  in children and adolescents
    de-awfulizing techniques and,
      34–35
    inappropriate interpretations and,
      31–32
    "Magnify" technique and, 34–35
    self-talk technique and, 33
  of culturally diverse clients, 53
  of clients with disabilities, 74–75
As. See Activating Events (As)
Attitude dimensions, toward disability,
    77–79
Authoritative virtuousness dimension,
    of disability attitude, 78–79
Avoidant personality disorder, REBT
    for, 170
Awfulizing
  de-awfulizing techniques and,
    34–35
  by clients with disabilities, 78, 92
  disputation strategy for, 57
  elegant solution and, 80–81
  in group therapy, 136
  irrational beliefs and, 18

B → C connection
  culturally diverse clients and, 44, 46,
    55
  of REBT therapy, 3
Borderline personality disorder, REBT
    for, 165

173

Case illustration of REBT
with children and adolescents, 6,
16–35
with client with disability, 7, 82,
88–98
with culturally diverse clients, 6,
56–62
with family as client, 111–128
with group client, 8, 153–156
Child and adolescent REBT
Activating Event assessment and,
15–16, 18
for anger disorders, 6, 29–31
for anxiety disorders, 6, 31–35
applications of, 14
case illustration of, 6
age-appropriate techniques and,
25–26
of anger, 29–31
anger and other-directed demands
and, 19–20
of anxiety, 31–35
Circle of Self activity and, 26
client cues and, 28–29
developmental level assessment
and, 25
disputation strategies and, 27–29
irrational beliefs assessment and,
18–21
negative self-rating and, 19, 22
parental involvement and, 22–23
practical vs. emotional problem
assessment and, 24
relevant examples use and, 27
therapeutic relationship and,
16–18
developmental level assessment and,
6, 14–15, 24–25
developmental stressors and, 12
getting vs. feeling better and, 15, 35
irrational beliefs assessment and,
15–16
parental involvement and, 15, 18,
22–23
practical vs. emotional problems and,
15, 23–24

prevalence of, 13
resource material on, 170
teaching and prevention emphasis
in, 13–14
therapeutic relationship and, 6,
15–18
confidentiality and, 17–18
direct questioning and, 20
listening without interrupting and,
18
parental involvement and, 18
selective labeling and, 20
Children with disabilities, 71–72
Circular causality concept
in family REBT treatment, 7,
101–103, 107–109
vs. linear causality, 101–102
Clients with disabilities, REBT with
bibliotherapy and, 81, 87
case illustration of, 7
ABC sequence and, 90–91
anger dissolution and, 82, 94–96
client introduction, 88–90
disputing beliefs, 92–93
initiating therapy, 90–91
making life changes and, 96
obstacles to therapy, 91
physical diagnosis and, 93–94
summary of, 97–98
therapy termination and, 96–97
client active collaboration and, 6–7
conclusions regarding, 98
discomfort anxiety and, 80
ego anxiety definition and, 80
elegant solution disputation strategy
and, 80–81, 84
factors affecting
attitudes toward disability, 77–79
cultural and religious beliefs, 76
disability type, 71
education and occupation, 73
emotional and cognitive resources,
75–76
onset age, 71–72, 77
onset type, 73
rehabilitation process, 73–75, 77

support system and living arrangements, 75
information sharing and, 81
irrational beliefs and, 74, 78–81, 89–90
 disputation of, 92–93
negative self-rating and, 79–80, 89–90, 92
positive aspects of, 79–81
special considerations for, 81
 assessment of presenting problem, 85
 bibliotherapy, 87
 disputation strategies, 86–87
 goal-setting, 86
 heterogeneity of disabilities, 83–84
 homework consequences, 87–88
 independence and identity issues, 82–83
 "insider-outsider" therapist attitude and, 79, 82
 self-acceptance, 84
 supportive vs. active-directive approaches, 84–85
 unconditional acceptance and, 84
therapist irrational beliefs and, 82–83
therapist negative biases and, 6, 79, 82
Cognitive homework in group REBT, 137
Cognitive-behavioral therapy
 for culturally diverse clients, 6
 B → C connection and, 44
 characteristics of, 43–44
 cultural congruence vs. incongruence concept and, 52
 empiricism and, 44
 vs. other therapies, 45
 stoicism and, 43–44
 "value-free" therapy concept and, 46
 for grief therapy, 165
 negative inferences challenged in, 4
 therapist interaction and, 151–152
 treatment outcome research and, 5
 See also Group REBT therapy

Congruence vs. incongruence, of cultural behavior, 52–53
Content therapy, definition of, 42–43
Countertransference and REBT group process, 143–144
Couples rational-emotive therapy, 167–168
Culturally diverse clients REBT with, 49–50
 B → C connection and, 45
 irrational beliefs and, 61–62
 case illustration of, 6
 client/therapist expectations and, 59
 cultural uniqueness and, 60–61
 disputation strategies and, 56–57
 initial session and, 58–60
 super ethnic issues and, 61–62
 cognitive-behavioral therapy and, 5, 6, 43–46
 conclusions regarding, 63
 congruence vs. incongruence concept and, 52–55
 "content" vs. "process" therapy concepts and, 42
 credibility and giving variables and, 41
 cultural uniqueness and
  as an Activating Event, 50–51
  client resistance potential and, 51
  definition of, 49–59
 disputation focus and, 56–57
 empiricism and, 44
 hedonic calculus for value clarification and, 51–52, 57
 hypothesis-testing skills and, 49
 irrational beliefs in, 56–57, 61–62
 literature review on, 39–41, 40n.1
 outcome variables and, 42
 reality data collection and, 55–56, 63
 sensitivity development and, 6, 41, 63
 Socratic approach and, 49
 stoicism and, 43–44
 super ethnic behavior and, 52, 61–62
 therapeutic imperialism concept and, 51–52

Culturally diverse clients REBT with
  (*continued*)
  therapist self-disclosure and, 48–49,
    53–55, 63
  therapist/client expectations and,
    44–45, 48–49, 54–55, 63
  traditional healing and, 56, 76
  Us *and* Them orientation and, 43–49
  Us *vs.* Them orientation and, 41–43
  within group heterogeneity and, 41
  Zen practitioners and, 47–48

Debate process, in REBT with families,
  110, 113–114, 124–125
Demandingness, irrational beliefs and,
  18
Depression
  of culturally diverse clients, 53
  of clients with disabilities, 74–75
  from negative self-rating, 20
  parental irrational beliefs and, 23
  REBT therapy for, 171
  of widowed clients, 164
Disabilities
  children with, 71–72
  vs. chronic illness, 70
  definition of, 70
  insider-outsider approach and, 79, 82
  "invisible disabilities" concept and,
    69, 71, 82
  prevalence of, 69
Discomfort anxiety
  of clients with disabilities, 80
  irrational beliefs and, 18
  irrational fears and, 20
  parental irrational beliefs and, 23
Disputation strategies
  anger payoffs and, 30–31
  for children and adolescents, 27–29
  for culturally diverse clients, 56–57
  for clients with disabilities, 80–81,
    86–87, 92–96
  "elegant solution" concept and,
    80–81, 84
  in group therapy, 132, 135–136, 139,
    153

philosophical disputing concept and,
  2
thought-stopping procedures and,
  92–93
Distraction technique, for clients with
  disabilities, 74

Eating disorders and REBT, 166
Ego anxiety, of clients with disabilities,
  80
"Elegant solution" concept, 80–81, 84
Empiricism, of REBT and cognitive-
  behavioral therapists, 44
Enactment process, in REBT with
  families, 113–115, 125–127
Encounter exercises in REBT groups,
  140
Encouragement in REBT groups, 140
Evaluative family beliefs, 103–105

Families, REBT with
  assessment and, 107–108
    A vs. A' clarification and, 109
    ABC vs. A'B'C' sequence and, 108,
      110–111, 113–115, 128
    circular causality and, 108–109
    complaints as goals and, 110–111,
      117–118
    exception times concept and,
      109–113
    family expectations and, 110–111
    of progress, 115–116
    unsuccessful solutions and, 111
  case illustration of
    ABC sequence and, 111–113,
      118–121
    A'B'C' sequence and, 121–124
    background information and,
      116–117
    complaints as goals and, 117–118
    conflict coping mechanisms and,
      104–105
    Debate process and, 124–125
    discussion of, 127–128
    Enactment process and, 125–127
  family beliefs and, 103

evaluative vs. non-evaluative,
104–105
importance of, 101
vs. individual beliefs, 127
"musturbatory" concept and, 107
primacy of, 128
rational and irrational beliefs and,
7, 105–106, 109, 112
family systems perspective and
circular causality and, 7, 101–103,
107–109
importance of, 101
traditional linear position and,
103
problem conceptualization and,
106–108
resource material on, 168
simultaneity concept and, 7
treatment strategies and
Debate process (D) and, 110,
113–114
Enactment (E) and, 113–115
homework assignments and, 114
Forceful coping self-statements and
REBT groups, 137–138, 154
Forceful taped disputing and REBT
groups, 139
Freud, Sigmund, 39

Gender differences, in mental health
misdiagnosis, 40
"Gloria" tape transcripts, 49n.3
Groups, REBT
behavioral techniques of
exposure to negative As, 140–141
penalties technique, 141
reinforcement technique, 141
relapse prevention, 141–142
skill training, 141
in vivo desensitization, 140
case illustration and, 8
paradoxical homework assignment
and, 155–156
rational-emotive imagery and,
154–155
Self-Help form and, 153

unconditional self-acceptance and,
155
cognitive techniques of
active disputing, 135–136
cognitive homework, 137
modeling, 137
negative self-rating and, 136, 145,
150–151
proselytizing, 137
psychoeducational methods, 137
rational coping self-statements, 136
recording sessions, 137
referenting, 136–137, 154
reframing, 137
conclusions regarding, 156–158
confidentiality issue and, 134–135
effectiveness of, 132–133
emotive techniques of
encounter exercises, 140
encouragement, 140
forceful taped disputing, 139
forceful coping self-statements,
137–138, 154
humor, 139
rational emotive imagery, 138, 154
relationship methods, 140
reverse role-playing, 138
role-playing, 138
homework assignments in, 132, 135,
137, 139, 144, 147, 149–150,
155–156
vs. individual therapy, 7
musturbatory concept in, 141–142,
142n.2, 149
participant selection for, 134–135
processes of
countertransference, 143–144
focusing on group processes,
145–149
intervention methods, 144–145
social skills training, 133, 140–141,
145, 154–156
therapist interaction and, 151–152
transference, 131, 142–143
unconditional acceptance, 143,
154–155

Groups, REBT *(continued)*
  processes of *(continued)*
    working with difficult members
      and, 149–151
    psychoanalytic deficiencies and,
      131–132
    regular session procedures and,
      135–136
    types of, 133–134

Healthy negative emotions vs. unhealthy
  negative emotions, 1, 138
Hedonic calculus, for value clarification,
  51–52, 57
Homework assignments
  for clients with disabilities, 87–88
  in family therapy, 114
  in group therapy, 132, 135, 137, 139,
    144, 147, 149–150, 155–156
Humor as intervention in REBT
  groups, 139

"I-can't-stand-it-itis" concept, 81, 136, 141
In vivo desensitization in REBT groups,
  140
Inferences
  about Activating Events, 4
  family beliefs as, 104
  of group clients, 136, 150
  negatively distorted, 5
"Insider-outsider" approach, and
  clients with disabilities, 79, 82
Instant Replay (Bedford), 31
"Invisible disabilities" concept, 69, 71, 82
Irrational beliefs
  absolutistic demands and evaluative
    conclusions of, 5
  alternative interpretations of, 4–5
  anger and other-directed demands
    and, 19–20
  in children and adolescents, 15
    assessment of, 18–20
    direct questioning and, 20
    low frustration tolerance and, 18, 20
    parent irrational beliefs and, 23
    selective labeling and, 20

specific feelings and, 21
  in culturally diverse clients, 56–57,
    61–62
  definition of, 105
  of clients with disabilities, 74, 78–81,
    89–90
  disputation strategies and, 92–96
  of families, 7, 105–106, 109, 112, 114
  in group therapy, 132
    homework assignments and, 135,
      149–150
    inferences and, 150–151
    reverse role-play and, 138
  philosophical disputing strategy and, 2
  vs. rational beliefs, 1, 105–106
  rational self-statements and, 2
  of therapist, 82–83, 86–87, 164
  See also Disputation strategies

Low frustration tolerance
  of clients with disabilities, 76
  group homework assignments and,
    135
  irrational beliefs and, 18, 20, 135
  REBT for, 171

Modeling in REBT groups, 137
Mouse, the Monster, and Me, The
  (Palmer), 31
Multicultural clients. *See* Culturally
  diverse clients REBT with
Musturbatory concept
  in family problem solving, 107
  in group therapy, 141–142, 142n.2, 149
  of phobic client, 165

Negative As, exposure to in REBT
  groups, 140–141
Negative self-rating
  Circle of Self activity and, 26
  depression from, 20
  of clients with disabilities, 79–80,
    89–90, 92–93
  of group clients, 136, 145, 150–151
  in guilt and depression, 3–4
  irrational beliefs and, 18–20

rational self-statements and, 2
self-acceptance and, 84
Nonevaluative family beliefs, 103–105

Panic attacks, REBT for, 169–170
Paradoxical homework assignment in
    REBT group, 155
Penalties in REBT groups, 141
Phobic client, REBT with, 165
"Post-Encounter" disability rehabilita-
    tion phase, 74
Post-traumatic stress disorder, REBT
    for, 165
"Pre-Encounter" disability rehabilitation
    phase, 74
Process therapy, definition of, 43
Proselytizing technique, 137, 164
Psychoanalysis
    deficiencies of, 131–132
    long-term vs. short-term outcome of,
        45
    vs. REBT, 2
    transference preoccupation of, 142
Psychoeducational techniques in REBT
    groups, 137
Psychological educators, 1
Psychotherapy
    and "content" therapy, 42
    for clients with disabilities, 75
    long-term vs. short-term outcome of,
        45
    philosophical basis of, 44

Rational beliefs
    definition of, 105
    vs. irrational beliefs, 1, 105–106
    rational coping self-statements and,
        136
Rational coping self-statements in
    REBT groups, 136
Rational emotive behavior therapy. *See*
    REBT
Rational emotive education therapy,
    165–166
Rational emotive imagery in REBT
    groups, 138, 154

Rational humorous songs, 139
Rational proselytizing, 164
"Rational-Reencounter" disability
    rehabilitation phase, 74
REBT
    features of
        B → C connection concept and, 3,
            44, 46
        client's description of A, therapist's
            acceptance of, 4
        ease of learning concepts, 1–2
        flexibility of, 2–3, 35
        results-orientation of, 3–4
    "Gloria" tape transcripts and,
        49n.3
    philosophical disputing in, 2
    vs. psychoanalysis, 2
    resources on, 164–172
    self-help group applications, 2
    Zen practitioners and, 47–48
    See also Child and adolescent REBT;
        Culturally diverse clients, REBT
        with; Clients with disabilities,
        REBT with; Families, REBT with;
        Groups, REBT with
Recording therapy sessions in REBT
    groups, 137
Referenting technique in REBT
    groups, 136–137, 154
Reframing technique
    for clients with disabilities, 74, 96
    for group REBT, 137
Reinforcement technique in REBT
    groups, 141
Relapse prevention technique in REBT
    groups, 141–142
Relationship methods in REBT groups,
    140
Reverse role-play technique in REBT
    groups, 138
Role-playing group technique in REBT
    groups, 138

Self-downing. *See* Negative self-rating
Social skills training in REBT groups,
    133, 140–141, 145, 154–156

Socratic approach
  with culturally diverse client, 49
  with client with disability, 85, 87
Stage theory, of rehabilitation process,
  74–75
Stoicism, in REBT and cognitive-
  behavioral therapies, 43–44
Substance abuse REBT for, 167, 171
Super ethnic behavior, 52, 61–62
Supportive rehabilitation approach,
  84–85

Therapeutic imperialism, definition of,
  51–52
Therapist activity level in REBT groups,
  151–152, 164

Transference
  group countertransference and,
    143–144
  group REBT process, 131, 142–143
  unconditional acceptance and, 143

Unconditional self-acceptance (USA) in
  REBT groups, 140, 143, 154–155
Unhealthy negative emotions vs.
  healthy negative emotions, 1, 138
"Universal fairness" irrational belief, of
  clients with disabilities, 78, 81

Widowed client, REBT with, 164

Zen practitioners, 47–48

$\mathbb{SP}$ *Springer Publishing Company*

The Practice of Rational Emotive Behavior Therapy
Second Edition
Albert Ellis, PhD, and Windy Dryden, PhD

This volume systematically reviews the practice of Rational Emotive Behavior Therapy and shows how it can be used by therapists in a variety of clinical settings. The book begins with an explanation of REBT as a general treatment model. It then addresses different treatment modalities, including individual, couple, family, and sex therapy.

The new edition modernizes the pioneering theories of Albert Ellis and contains a complete updating of references over the past ten years. The authors have added new information on teaching the principles of unconditional self-acceptance in a structured, group setting. With extensive use of actual case examples to illustrate each of the different settings, this volume will appeal to clinical and counseling psychologists as well as any other helping professionals involved in therapy.

Contents:

The General Theory of REBT • The Basic Practice of REBT • A Case Illustration of the Basic Practice of REBT: The Case of Jane • Individual Therapy • Couples Therapy • Family Therapy • Group Therapy • Rational Emotive Behavior Marathons and Intensives • Teaching the Principles of Unconditioned Self-Acceptance in a Structured Group Setting • The Rational Emotive Behavioral Approach to Sex Therapy • The Use of Hypnosis with REBT • How to Maintain and Enhance Your Rational Emotive Behavior Therapy Gains

1997   280pp   0-8261-5471-9   hardcover

536 Broadway, New York, NY 10012-3955 • (212) 431-4370 • Fax (212) 941-7842

⑤ *Springer Publishing Company*

Brief But Comprehensive Psychotherapy
The Multimodal Way

Arnold A. Lazarus, PhD, ABPP

The current healthcare environment has created a need for short-term, time-limited, cost-effective and brief forms of psychotherapy, emphasizing efficiency and efficacy. The central message is "don't waste time." But how can one be brief and also comprehensive?

In his latest addition to the psychotherapy literature, the prestigious Arnold Lazarus modernizes his eclectic and goal-oriented approach to psychotherapy. Dr. Lazarus employs and transcends customary methods of diagnosis and treatment by providing several distinctive assessment procedures and therapeutic recommendations.

Using his traditional acronym — BASIC ID — he stresses the assessment of seven dimensions of a client's personality: behavior, affect, sensation, imagery, cognition, interpersonal relationships, and the need for drugs. This volume contains many ideas that will augment and enhance the skills and clinical repertoires of every therapist.

Contents:

Let's Cut to the Chase? • Elucidating the Main Rationale • What is the Multimodal Way? • Theories and Techniques • Assessment Procedures Employed Only by Multimodal Therapists (Part One: Bridging and Tracking) • Assessment Procedures Employed Only by Multimodal Therapists (Part Two: Second-Order Basic ID and Structural Profiles) • Some Elements of Effective Brevity • Activity and Serendipity • Two Specific Applications: Problems of Sexual Desire and the Treatment of Dysthymia • Couples Therapy • Some Common Time Wasters

Springer Series on Behavior Therapy and Behavioral Medicine
1997   196 pp   0-8261-9640-3   hardcover

536 Broadway, New York, NY 10012-3955 • (212) 431-4370 • Fax (212) 941-7842

 **Springer Publishing Company**

Stress Counseling
A Rational Emotive Behavior Approach
Albert Ellis, Jack Gordon, Michael Neenan, and Stephen Palmer

This book is a comprehensive study of the theory and practice of the Rational Emotive Behavior Therapy approach applied to counseling and psychotherapy with patients coping with stress. The distinguished authors provide case studies and client examples and client exercises to assist clinicians in both individual and group therapy.

Recognizing that their clearly laid out programs may need to be altered for specific clients, further information is provided on occupational stress, crisis intervention, brief psychotherapy situations, and difficult clients. With extensive appendices and resource lists, and material on techniques such as skills training, relaxation methods, hypnosis and biofeedback, this book is appropriate for practitioners, educators and trainees in clinical and occupational settings.

Contents:
- Stress: A REBT Perspective
- Assessment in REBT
- The Beginning Stage of Stress Counseling
- The Middle Stage of Stress Counseling
- The Ending Stage of Stress Counseling
- Additional Techniques for Stress Counseling With REBT
- Brief Psychotherapy with Crisis Intervention in REBT
- How to Deal With Difficult Clients
- Occupational Stress and Group Work
- Afterword: Training in REBT

1997   200pp   0-8261-1163-7   softcover

536 Broadway, New York, NY 10012-3955 • (212) 431-4370 • Fax (212) 941-7842

⑤ *Springer Publishing Company*

The Essential Albert Ellis
Seminal Writings on Psychotherapy
Windy Dryden, PhD, Editor

This insightful new book gathers a selection of Ellis' most important writings in one concise resource. The text includes an introduction providing a brief review of the development of Ellis' thought, and serves to place the successive articles in context. The Essential Albert Ellis is therefore both a convenient reference for knowledgeable professionals and a helpful guide for students.

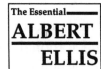

The Essential——
ALBERT
ELLIS
Seminal Writings ——
on Psychotherapy
Windy Dryden
Editor

Springer Publishing Company

Partial Contents:
- The General Theory of Rational-Emotive Therapy (RET)
- Toward a Theory of Personality
- The Biological Basis of Human Irrationality
- Psychotherapy and the Value of a Human Being
- Discomfort Anxiety:
  A New Cognitive-Behavioral Construct
- Is RET "Rationalist" of "Constructivist"
- The Basic Practice of RET
- Intimacy in RET
- The Use of Rational Humorous Songs in Psychotherapy
- The Issue of Force and Energy in Behavioral Change
- The Value of Efficiency in Psychotherapy
- Failures in Rational-Emotive Therapy
- Rational-Emotive Therapy Approaches to
  Overcoming Resistance
- How to Deal with Your Most Difficult Client —You

1990   336pp   0-8261-6940-6   hardcover

536 Broadway, New York, NY 10012-3955 • (212) 431-4370 • Fax (212) 941-7842